Contents

Fatal Forces

Introduction   7

Nasty Newton   11

Forceful facts   28

Smashing speed   38

Gruesome gravity   54

Under pressure   71

Facts about friction   82

Stretching and straining   97

Getting in a spin   107

Bouncing back   125

Mighty machines   136

Build or bust   146

May the forces be with you   159

The Fight For Flight

Introduction   165

Death-defying flying facts   168

Big-brained bird men and   183
plunging parachutes

Barmy balloons   201

Awesome airships   220

The Wright way to invent the plane   227

Plane-crazy planes   249

Potty pioneer pilots   271

Jumping jets   284

Epilogue: fateful flight   301

FATAL FORCES

Nick Arnold has been writing stories and books since he was a youngster, but never dreamt he'd find fame writing about Horrible Science. His research involved lying on a bed of nails and making a parachute jump and he enjoyed every minute of it.

When he's not delving into Horrible Science, he spends his spare time teaching adults in a college. His hobbies include eating pizza, riding his bike and thinking up corny jokes (though not all at the same time).

Tony De Saulles picked up his crayons when he was still in nappies and has been doodling ever since. He takes Horrible Science very seriously and even agreed to test what happens when your parachute doesn't open. Fortunately, his injuries weren't too serious.

When he's not out with his sketchpad, Tony likes to write poetry and play squash, though he hasn't written any poetry about squash yet.

Introduction

Science has one fatal flaw. It can be **seriously** boring. Ask a simple question and you're forced to listen to a really boring, complicated answer.

WHY DOES MY BALL FALL?

THE FORCE OF GRAVITATIONAL ATTRACTION BETWEEN YOUR SPHERICAL OBJECT AND THE EARTH IS DETERMINED BY THEIR RELATIVE MASSES. *1

YER-WOT?

Some answers have masses of mysterious mathematics…

BUT WHY DOES IT FALL SO *FAST*?

SIMPLE – 9.806 METRES PER SECOND = $g = Gm_2/r^2$ *2

TOTALLY BAMBOOZLED

7

And don't try arguing with a scientist either…

Or you'll get a forceful reply…

See what I mean? It's enough to make you die of boredom. Now that *would* be fatal.

* English translations:

1 Gravity is the force that pulls things down towards the Earth. The same force pulls a smaller object towards a much larger object.

2 The speed the ball falls depends on the strength of gravity. And this depends on the size of the Earth and your distance from the Earth's centre.

3 You're asking too many questions. I'll try blinding you with science.

So what are these laws? And what happens if you break them? Do you get expelled? Or perhaps there's a *really horrible* punishment in store for you. Maybe you'll be *forced* to endure extra science lessons with megatons of homework? And who *forces* you to obey these horrible laws anyway? Teachers? No.

WELL WHAT'S FORCING ME TO FALL, THEN?

Forces force you. Because forces force things to move. And a force can be anything from you flicking a pea, to the awesome gravity of a giant star. So the effects of forces can be an inter-galactic explosion or the pea ending up in your teacher's ear-hole. (This might cause an explosion too!)

But forces can have fascinating fatal effects. Like crushing people, or making them sick, or pulling their heads off. (Getting forces wrong at school isn't usually quite as fatal – just a bit of en-forced detention from your teacher.)

CRUNCH!

ARGHH!

THAT MUST BE ONE OF THOSE HORRIBLE FORCES YOU WERE TELLING US ABOUT, SIR

So here's the real-life story of forces. It's a story involving fatal fortunes and horrible happenings. And it's all true. And who knows? Afterwards you might feel that forces have a fatal attraction for you, too. You might even force your teacher to take your science homework seriously. If you can just force yourself to read the next page now…

Nasty  Newton

The prisoner was sick. In the madness of his fever he imagined the courtroom candles were fiery ghosts. Again and again he heard the sentence of the judges: "Death!" Then he fainted.

He awoke in darkness. Dragging himself upright he tried to explore the pitch black cell. His feet slithered on the slimy floor. Then he stumbled, his hands grabbing at empty air. He'd collapsed on the edge of a bottomless pit. One more step and he'd have dropped like a stone. Exhausted, the prisoner fell asleep. But when he awoke he found himself strapped to a low bench. Helpless, he peered upwards and gasped in horror.

A giant statue towered over him. The grotesque figure had a huge pendulum swinging from its hands. The pendulum swung to and fro with an evil hiss. It ended in a razor-sharp blade and each slow sweep brought the blade a little lower. A little closer. Hiss … hiss … HISSSSSS! Scores of huge rats stared hungrily from the shadows, waiting to feast on the prisoner's butchered corpse. The deadly hissing blade skimmed his bare chest…

DON'T PANIC! It's only a story – *The Pit and the Pendulum* was written in 1849 by the American author Edgar Alan Poe. But for scientists Poe's story has a fatal fascination. The nasty forms of death – the pit and the pendulum – involve forces. Falling into the well under the influence of gravity; the pendulum's swing controlled by gravity and centripetal force (see page 108). (That's the force on the pendulum shaft that stops the swinging weight pulling away from the rest of the machine.) These forces are fatal for the prisoner.

HORRIBLE HEALTH WARNING!

Forces aren't human. You can't reason with them or persuade them. They are physical forces of nature with the power to kill. Fatal forces. Once you fall foul of fatal forces you're FINISHED!

Postscript:

Oh – by the way you'll be pleased to know the prisoner escapes. How? By getting the rats to gnaw through his straps, of course. Bet you didn't think of that! Amazingly enough these forces had already been explained by a forceful scientific mega-star, the amazing Sir Isaac Newton.

Hall of fame: Sir Isaac Newton (1642–1727)
Nationality: British

Isaac Newton was born on Christmas Day. The doctor thought baby Isaac wouldn't live because he was so weak and small.

But Isaac survived. He soon became interested in science but his teachers didn't think he was especially brainy. In fact, Isaac was too busy performing experiments at home to work hard at school. (Don't try this excuse.) When young Isaac was 16 his mum asked him to run the family farm. But he proved to be a useless farmer. He spent all his time experimenting and allowed the sheep to guzzle their way through a cornfield.

HE WAS THE BEST FARMER WE EVER HAD!

So Isaac went to Cambridge University instead. At University he read every maths book he could find. (Including the ones without pictures.) He wore scruffy clothes and was so absent-minded he often got lost on his way to supper. As far as Isaac was concerned supper was for wimps. Who needed supper when you could do lovely science calculations instead?

INCREDIBLY DIFFICULT MATHS

In 1665 a deadly plague struck London. Soon 7,000 people were dying every week and the authorities closed Cambridge University to stop the plague spreading. So Isaac went home. But instead of taking a holiday he did *extra homework*. Very strange. But what homework! He invented calculus – a mathematical system still used today to plan rocket trips, and he also discovered that light contains colours.

These vital discoveries were to influence maths and physics for 300 years. Then Isaac made a *really* incredible breakthrough…

The apple and the moon

Woolsthorpe, England 1666

It was getting dark, but the skinny young man ran his fingers through his shoulder-length hair and carried on reading. Isaac Newton was sitting in the orchard trying to figure out how the moon went round the Earth. Suddenly a call rang out from the old farmhouse:

"Hmm," thought Isaac, "she always calls me half-an-hour *before* supper. It's a trick to get me in on time."

So he did nothing. If he had left the orchard when his mother called him the entire history of science would have been different. But just then something grabbed his attention.

It had been waiting for this moment. Waiting for months, silently. At first it was no larger than a tiny green bulge. But now it was bright red and the size of a man's fist. A living bubble of water and sugars with sweet juicy flesh and bitter seeds all wrapped in a waxy skin. An apple. The most famous apple in science.

"Isaac! Your supper's on the table and it's your favourite!"

"Coming, mother!"

Isaac shivered as a cool breeze rustled the trees. Then he sighed and reluctantly closed his book. There was a silent snap. The slender stalk holding the apple to the tree gave way. Wrenched by an unseen force the apple hurtled downward. It tumbled through the rustling leaves and bounced gently on Isaac's brainy bonce.

16

What would you have done? Perhaps you'd have eaten your supper and forgotten the apple. But Isaac wasn't like that. He rubbed his head and looked at the moon. It shone like a bright silver coin in the evening sky.

"So why doesn't the moon fall, too?" he asked himself, as he absent-mindedly munched the famous apple.

For some strange reason Isaac remembered his school and the dreaded "bucket game". He hated the other kids for making him play. He remembered having to whirl a bucket of water around his head on a rope. It was hard work and Isaac was a thin little boy. But amazingly all the water had stayed in the bucket as if trapped by an unseen force.

"Maybe that's what keeps the moon in place," he murmured.

Then his mother shouted again: "Isaac, your supper's on the table and it's stone cold."

"I said I'm coming, mother!"

As Isaac threw the apple away he wondered what would happen if it reached the moon. The most famous apple core in science disappeared. There was a muffled meow as it splatted on the cat.

Isaac had forgotten his supper. He was calculating how strong gravity would need to be to stop the apple sailing into space. Then he thought about how fast the moon has to move to prevent it crashing down to Earth.

Later a very annoyed Mrs Newton stood in the doorway shielding her candle from the cold night air.

"Isaac!" she yelled. "I've fed your supper to the cat. And I'm going to feed your breakfast to the pigs!"

There was no answer from the orchard. But Isaac was still out there. And still thinking hard.

Test your teacher

How much does your teacher really know about this famous scientist?

1 As a child what was Isaac Newton's favourite toy?

a) A chemistry set.

b) A toy windmill powered by a mouse in a wheel.

c) He hated toys. He preferred tricky maths sums.

2 What did he buy on his first day at university?

a) A desk, ink and a notebook for extra homework.

b) New clothes and a ticket to the local fun fair.

c) A loaf of bread to eat.

3 How did Newton solve tricky scientific problems?

a) The answers came in a flash of inspiration when Newton was on the toilet.

b) By talking things over with scientific friends.

c) Worrying away at the problem day and night until he figured out the answer.

4 Newton became Professor of Mathematics at Cambridge but no one attended his bum-numbingly boring lectures.

So what did he do?

a) He rounded up students and *forced* them to listen.

b) Carried on talking to an empty room.

c) Tried to make his lectures interesting with a few jokes and amusing stories.

5 Newton's dog knocked over a candle and 20 years hard work went up in flames. What did he do?

a) Drew his sword and killed the dog.

b) Re-wrote his work from memory.

c) Forgot about the old work and studied something new and experimental.

Answers:

1 b) He designed it himself. **2 a)**, **3 c)**, **4 b)** Does your teacher have this problem? **5 b)**.

What your teacher's score means.

1-2 Your teacher's guessing.

3-4 Your teacher knows a bit but doesn't know everything. (Much like any other teacher.)

5 Hard luck. Your teacher's read this book.

Newton's moving book

Newton didn't publish his discoveries for 20 years. He was too busy with his mathematical work. But then at

19

last, fearful others might grab the glory, Newton wrote a book about his ideas. He shut himself away for 18 months and worked 20 hours a day.

Sometimes Newton's assistant reminded him that he'd missed supper.

"Have I?" Newton would murmur sleepily. Then he nibbled at the food and got back to work.

THE CARROT WAS FOR YOUR SUPPER, SIR

Newton's book was called *The Philosophiae Naturalis Principia Mathematica* and it was the most brilliant science book ever written. In it he explained the whole universe in a way that made sense. (Well – it would have made sense if the book hadn't been in Latin and filled with mystifying maths.) Newton described gravity and three crucial laws about forces and how things move. These laws show how squids squirt water backwards in order to move forwards. They explain what happens when distant stars blow up and why low-flying sparrow droppings splat on your head.

CHAPTER 47 BEWARE OF LOW-FLYING BIRDS

One way to imagine Newton's laws is to think of a really horrible morning. What d'you mean – every day's like that?

Newton's First Law

> *What the law says...*
> *If left alone a motionless object doesn't move. A moving object carries on moving in a straight line at a constant speed as long as another force doesn't make it change course.*

What the Law means...

You stare wearily at your breakfast. Your cornflakes are motionless and they're going to stay that way until you summon up the energy to eat them. You clumsily knock your spoon and half your breakfast goes flying. A cornflake falls on your dad's head. The cornflake would have flown in the same direction for ever but the force of gravity pulled it down.

CORNFLAKE WOULD TRAVEL IN A STRAIGHT LINE FOR EVER IF IT WASN'T FOR THE FORCE OF GRAVITY (AND THE CEILING).

OOPS! SORRY DAD!

DOWNWARD FORCE OF THE HAND CATAPULTS THE CORNFLAKE UPWARDS

Newton's Second Law

What the law says...
When a force is applied to an object
it changes its momentum. The force
moves the object in the same direction
as the force is moving, at a speed
proportional to the strength of this force.

What the Law means…
That's why the force of a hefty kick can send a football
whizzing towards a goalie at a deadly speed.

Newton's Third Law

What the law says...
When an object exerts a force on
another object the second object will
push back just as hard.

What the Law means...

You're late and you're jogging to school. But you're still not properly awake. You slam into a lamppost. And the lamppost wallops you back! It's true – this really does happen.

Bet you never knew!

When Newton's apple hit the ground the Earth bumped against the apple. That's what Newton's Third Law says: things always push back with equal force. But the Earth moved such a tiny distance no one noticed. Oddly enough a unit of force was later named the "Newton" in the scientist's honour. And the weight produced by one Newton is roughly the same as ... an apple. But Newton was no ordinary genius. He had a nasty side, too.

Newton's nasty nature

1 When Newton was three years old his mum remarried. Isaac hated his stepfather and often thought of killing him. He didn't of course, but he was pleased when the stepfather died.

2 At school Newton had no friends until he thumped the school bully with great force. Newton was smaller than his opponent but his cunning helped win the fight. After this nasty incident Newton became popular.

3 Newton disliked women and never married. He hated his friend John Locke's attempts to introduce him to ladies. Later Newton wrote to Locke:

when (a woman) told me you were sickly and would not live, I answered t'were better you were dead

THANKS A LOT!

But that didn't stop Newton generously allowing his niece Catherine to do his cooking and cleaning.

4 Newton was a miserable man. He had no hobbies apart from work. He rarely laughed and he called poetry:

A KIND OF INGENIOUS NONSENSE

5 In 1686 Newton fell out with scientist Robert Hooke (1635–1703). Hooke unjustly accused Newton of pinching *his* ideas on gravity. In a letter Newton called Hooke "a pretender and a grasper" and refused to talk to him.

6 After writing the *Principia* Newton had a nasty turn. He went mad for two years and did no scientific research. Some historians reckon Newton was a bit depressed but others say he was poisoned by the mercury he used for chemistry experiments.

7 When he got better Newton was appointed Warden of the Royal Mint and reformed Britain's coinage. It was said that nasty Newton enjoyed catching forgers and sending them to their executions.

I WILL NOW DEMONSTRATE ANOTHER OF THE FATAL FORCES...

8 German Gottfried Leibniz (1646–1716) claimed he invented calculus. Newton accused Leibniz of pinching his idea. But in fact Leibniz had made the discovery independently at the same time as Newton. (And it was Leibniz who actually coined the word "calculus" – Newton called it "fluxions" – which sounds like the effects of a nasty tummy bug.)

9 Newton came to a horrible end. He moved to the country to improve his health. But a few weeks later he fell sick and died of a stone in his bladder. By then, however, he was a nasty-tempered old man of 84, but still a great genius.

Newton in his own words

Like many geniuses Newton was hard to understand.
Here's what he said about himself:

Note: Newton didn't mean human pyramids. The giants
he referred to were earlier scientists who inspired him.
He also said:

Note: Newton meant that he'd learnt enough to realize there was more to learn. He was right. He'd only scratched the surface. There are loads more fatally fascinating facts about forces. You'll find them in the next chapter.

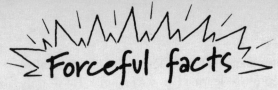

Forceful facts

Forces are everywhere. You can't do much without bumping into them. But hopefully not with a fatal *CRUNCH*. Oddly enough, though, before Newton, people knew very little about how forces worked.

Mixed-up motion theories

A scientist will tell you that a force is something that affects the movement or shape of an object or person. Sounds fairly vague. But before Newton, scientific theories were even more mixed-up. One of the first people to write about forces was a Greek genius called Aristotle.

Hall of fame: Aristotle (384–322 BC) Nationality: Greek

Aristotle was a doctor's son. His parents died when he was a child and as a young man he blew their money on wild parties. But when he was 17 years old Aristotle had a sudden change of heart and sent himself back to school.

WEIRD! I SUDDENLY FEEL LIKE DOING LOADS OF HOMEWORK!

He went to study under the brainy philosopher called Plato in the Academy at Athens. Aristotle liked it there so much that he stayed for the next 20 years as a pupil and then as a teacher.

Aristotle travelled for four years and eventually moved to Macedonia where his old mate Philip happened to be king. Phil asked Aristotle to teach his boy, Alexander. Aristotle must have done a good job because young Alexander became Alexander the Great and conquered a great chunk of Asia. By the time Aristotle died (of acute indigestion) he had written about everything from politics to how grasshoppers chirp. And he even had a few things to say about forces.

Mystery motions

Here's how Aristotle explained forces:

Wrong, wrong and wrong again. But for 2,000 years everyone thought Aristotle's wacko ideas were RIGHT. Eventually Newton used maths to prove Aristotle WRONG. So nowadays we've got forces sussed. As a scientist might say, "Learning about forces is as easy as riding a bike." Oh, yeah? Riding a bike is LOADS harder and just to prove it we've asked a scientist to try.

Scientific cycling in ten easy lessons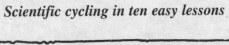

THE SMALL PRINT:
IT'S NOT OUR FAULT IF YOU END UP IN HOSPITAL – O.K.?

Lesson 1: Wobbly balance

Remember learning to ride a bike? Tough, wasn't it? Inside the scientist's ears are fluid-filled spaces, called semi-circular canals. (Teachers have a larger air-filled space where their brains should be. Ha ha.) These canals help her balance on two wheels. As the liquid sloshes around, sensors tell her brain whether she's still upright. Her brilliant brain also notices the force of gravity, her speed, the slope and wind direction. Yep – all at the same time.

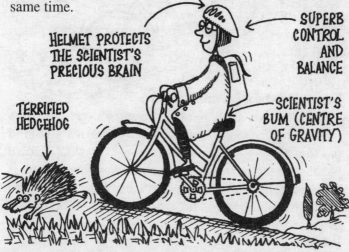

HELMET PROTECTS THE SCIENTIST'S PRECIOUS BRAIN

SUPERB CONTROL AND BALANCE

TERRIFIED HEDGEHOG

SCIENTIST'S BUM (CENTRE OF GRAVITY)

It helps her balance if her science books, sandwiches, etc. aren't draped over one handlebar. Ideally her bum is the centre of gravity – the point around which everything else is sensibly balanced.

Lesson 2: Effortless inertia

Inertia means that things at rest tend to stay put. That's why it takes more energy to start cycling than to keep going. But our scientist has got to start somewhere. So she gets peddling and once she's moving it's easier to carry on. Inertia helps her keep going in a straight line. But she still needs a bit more peddling and puffing. Phew!

OH DEAR! THE HILL SEEMS TO HAVE GOT A BIT STEEPER

PUFF! GASP!

HILLS REQUIRE MORE ENERGY

SCIENTIST HAS TO PUSH DOWN HARDER ON THE PEDALS

Lesson 3: Mass-ive momentum

Momentum is a measure of the scientist's ability to keep going. And her momentum depends on her mass. If your reaction to this statement is to say "yer wot?", you'd better read the next bit. Mass means how much there is of the scientist – everything in her body, her clothes and even what she had for breakfast. His mass, her bike's mass and her speed combine to produce her momentum. Wheee!

WHEEEE

NO NEED TO PEDAL

WHOOSH

NOT AGAIN!

Lesson 4: Mixed-up momentum

Oops! She knocks the school bully flying. Scientists would say she's "transferred momentum" to the bully and call this "conserving momentum". The posh scientific word for speed in one direction is "velocity". So she'd better pedal at quite a velocity in order to conserve her life!

TRANSFER OF MOMENTUM
TAKES PLACE HERE

BAD

BULLY LANDS
SOMEWHERE
OVER HERE

Oo-er the bully's heading towards her on a skateboard. THEY'RE GOING TO CRASH! As they crash the two momentums cancel each other. So they both grind to a halt. Result = TROUBLE!!!

Lesson 5: Galloping gravity

Velocity is greater when cycling downhill. Gravity tries to pull the scientist to the centre of the Earth. And the bottom of the slope is a bit nearer the centre of the planet than the top. This explains why, if she loses her balance, it's easier to fall off her bike than stay on. By the way, if she did make it right through to the Earth's centre, the gravity would be strong enough to squash her into a fleshy ball. Yikes!

Tired yet? Our scientist is. She's run out of kinetic energy. That's the posh scientific name for the energy she uses when moving. Oh well – we'll give her a few minutes to recover and then we'll put her back to work.

Lesson 6: Awkward acceleration and drag

For the scientist the word "acceleration" means changing speed or direction. So even when she slows down, she calls it "acceleration". But when she accelerates down a hill she feels the wind whistling up her nostrils (and everywhere else), and trying to slow her. This force is called "drag". If it's particularly windy it'll "drag" her off her bike – the result could be fatal.

Lesson 7: Careering centrifugal force

Rounding a corner too fast can be fatal too. The scientist leans into the corner because her bike wants to continue in a straight line. If she tries not to lean – she'll probably fall off. This effect is known as "centrifugal force". If she simply turned the handlebars her bike's centrifugal force would chuck her in the opposite direction.

SCIENTIST LEANS THIS WAY →

TO STOP CENTRIFUGAL FORCE PUSHING HER OVER THIS WAY ←

Lesson 8: Grinding gears

The gears on the scientist's bike help her cycle uphill. The gears turn the wheels slower than her pedalling. This means the pedalling isn't such hard work. When she zooms downhill at a higher speed she can use a higher gear to pedal more slowly but with greater force. Yep – gears are great. As a scientist would say, "They're a great way of transferring forces."

Lesson 9: Furious friction

The force of friction slows moving objects. It happens when a moving object touches another object. The scientist's rubber tyres grip the road and provide this force. This helps her control the bike and avoid fatal collisions. Lack of friction makes cycling on ice a slippery experience. And performing wheelies on the local skating rink is definitely out.

When she wants to slow down, or stop the rubber brakes grip her wheels and friction stops her bike. Hopefully. If she brakes too hard, her momentum throws her forward. And she performs spectacular but possibly fatal handlebar acrobatics.

Lesson 10: Vicious vibrations

When the scientist rides her bike along a bumpy path she may feel a few vibrations. These are shock waves carrying the force of impact from the tyres. Her tyres and saddle springs are designed to soak up some vibrations. But that doesn't stop her body vibrating, her muscles twitching and her eyeballs bouncing slightly in their sockets.

Freaky physicists

Scientists who study forces are called physicists (*fizzy-sists*). They also explore motion, probe what things are made of, and try to figure out how the universe works. A typical physicist is slightly scruffy and enjoys tinkering with things. A physics lab is rather untidy and full of interesting bits and pieces that have been salvaged in order to build a freaky machine.

Fatal expressions

WE'VE MAXIMIZED OUR POTENTIAL ENERGY!

Is this dangerous?

Answer: Just a bit. It means that when the roller-coaster goes to the top of a slope it's built up a lot of potential energy that will allow it to rush down the other side.

Bet you never knew!

Physicists use two strange words in connection with forces – "energy" and "work". Well hopefully, they don't sound too strange to you. But we're not talking about summoning up the energy to do homework or wash the dishes here. No way.

Physicists say "work" when they want to explain what happens when a force causes an object to move a distance. According to them writing your maths homework is "work" but reckoning up the answers in your head isn't. Energy is the ability to do work. Sounds sensible – after all you need energy to work. Don't you?

Just thinking about energy and work is pretty exhausting isn't it, so why don't you take a little rest? Yeah – put your feet up. Get your breath back for the next chapter. You'll need it. 'Cos it's about speed and crashes!!! Fasten your safety belt.

Smashing speed

Some people think speed is smashing. Others don't. Early railways scared some people because they reckoned no human could go faster than 32 km per hour (20 mph) and live. Well, they can, of course. But one thing's certain – the faster you go the more likely you are to meet up with some fatal forces. Gulp!

Test your teacher

Is your teacher quick-witted? Smile sweetly and ask:

WHAT WAS THE FASTEST SPEED ATTAINED ON A BICYCLE DURING THE NINETEENTH CENTURY?

(Note the subtle wording – your teacher probably thinks you're talking about pedalling – but she'd be wrong.)

Your teacher will probably say something like, "50 km per hour" (31 mph) – hopelessly wrong. At this point you can say, "No, I think you're wrong. In 1899 Mr C. M. Murphy smashed the record. He tied his bike to the back of a train and travelled 1.6 km (1 mile) in a minute."
Don't try this at home.

Quick quiz

1 Super speedy

See if you can put these three objects in order of speed, starting with the fastest.

a) A bullet from a high-powered rifle.

b) The planet Mercury moving through space.

c) Three astronauts aboard the Apollo 10 spacecraft in 1969.

2 Fairly speedy

Which of these three objects do you think is the fastest?

a) A chameleon's tongue as it grabs a juicy fly.

b) A message sent along one of your nerves.

c) A person falling from the top of a 99.4 metre-high building.

3 Slow and sluggish

Can you put these three objects in order of speed starting with the fastest?

a) Your fingernails growing.

b) Bamboo plants growing.

c) The Atlantic Ocean getting wider.

Answers:

1 b) 172,248 km per hour (107,030 mph) When it comes to orbiting the sun, Mercury is the speediest planet in the solar system. **c)** 39,897 km per hour (24,791 mph) Feeling a teensy bit space sick? **a)** 3,302 km per hour (2,052 mph). That's too fast to see. The bullet travels faster than sound so a person could be shot before they heard the gun firing. Doesn't sound fair somehow.

2 b) 483 km per hour (300 mph). **c)** 141 km per hour (80 mph). This was the speed achieved by stuntman Dan Koko in 1984 as he leapt off the Las Vegas World Hotel. Lucky for Dan he smashed into an air cushion rather than the pavement. **a)** 80.5 km per hour (50 mph). Then it's bye-bye fly.

3 b) 3 cm an hour. If your fingernails grew any faster than this, you'd have problems. **c)** 0.0006 cm an hour. The Atlantic Ocean is getting wider due to the movements of enormous slabs of rock deep beneath the Earth's surface. **a)** 0.00028 cm an hour. Any faster than this and it could be fatal.

Bet you never knew!

You'd move faster if your shape allowed the air to flow round you rather than bumping into you. This kind of shape is called "aerodynamic" and it cuts down on drag. A bullet with its pointed head is an aerodynamic shape but a human head isn't. If it was we'd all have pointy heads. Record-smashing speed cyclists wear pointed helmets instead. And more speed means more momentum. Smashing!

NAME: Momentum

THE BASIC FACTS: Momentum keeps you moving. That way you don't smash Newton's First Law. (That's the one about going in a straight line unless something stops you.)

THE HORRIBLE DETAILS: Momentum makes your stomach jump when you go over the top on a roller coaster.

ARGHHHH!

The momentum of your half-digested food carries on up. If it comes up too far it could be fatally embarrassing!

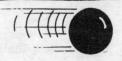

Murderous momentum facts

1 In 1871 showman John Holtum tried to catch a flying cannon-ball *with his bare hands*. It wasn't fired from a real cannon, of course. Holtum used a specially built gun that fired a slow-moving ball. But even so he nearly lost a finger. The stunt proved very popular and John bravely practised until he'd perfected the trick. He should have changed his name to "Halt-em".

2 In nineteenth-century America railways were rarely fenced off and brainless buffalo often blundered onto the tracks. To tackle this menace, by the 1860s trains were fitted with wedge-shaped "cow catchers". The idea was that the train's momentum would scoop the buffalo out of harm's way.

3 In Finland, elk (otherwise known as moose) cause fatal road accidents. When hit by a car, the momentum of the car flips the moose over. So the loose moose lands on the car roof. Its weight crushes both the car and its driver. Perhaps the cars should be fitted with "moose catchers".

Idle inertia

Physicists use the word inertia to describe how things stay the same. Motionless things stay idle and moving things carry on until another force gets in the way. That's Newton's First Law again.

Dare you discover … the inertia of an egg?

What you need:
A plate
A raw egg
A hard-boiled egg

What you do:

1 Gently spin the raw egg on the plate.

2 To stop the egg touch it with your finger.

3 Gently lift your finger up.

4 Now repeat steps 1-3 with the hard-boiled egg.

What do you notice?

a) When you lift your finger the hard-boiled egg continues to spin.

b) When you lift your finger the raw egg continues to spin.

c) When you lift your finger the raw egg spins and the hard-boiled egg rocks from end-to-end.

DON'T PUSH DOWN TOO HARD

WHOOPS

Answer:
b) When you stop the raw egg, inertia keeps the egg white inside spinning. And this starts the entire egg spinning again when you lift your finger. The inside of the hard-boiled egg is hard, of course, so the white doesn't have its own inertia.

Important note: The egg should spin on the plate. Not spin through the air and smash on the floor. If this happens you'll be force-fed omelette. And talking about smashing things...

43

A smashing test

Car designers spend fortunes building new cars. And then they smash them up. This may sound stupid, but they need to test the car's structural design and materials under crash conditions and also find the best ways to ensure that the driver and passengers are as well protected as possible. These days most smashes happen on a computer screen. The engineers peer at a simulation of crashes at various speeds. They can even slow down the movement to one image every two milliseconds – that's far slower than a TV action replay.

But afterwards the engineers need real-life tests to check their findings. And this is when the poor old dummies get wheeled in to show the effects of the crash on real people. Of course, dummies don't have brains – that's why they're dummies. But they do have a smashing time.

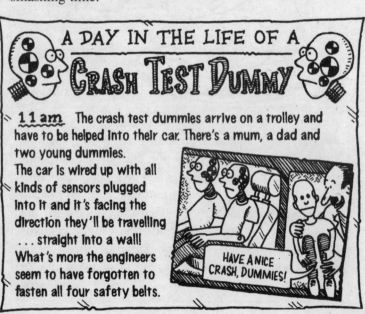

A DAY IN THE LIFE OF A
CRASH TEST DUMMY

11 am The crash test dummies arrive on a trolley and have to be helped into their car. There's a mum, a dad and two young dummies.

The car is wired up with all kinds of sensors plugged into it and it's facing the direction they'll be travelling ... straight into a wall! What's more the engineers seem to have forgotten to fasten all four safety belts.

HAVE A NICE CRASH, DUMMIES!

11.02 am The engineers crouch behind steel barriers to protect themselves from the impact of the crash, and it turns out they *deliberately* forgot about the safety belts. Steel cables at the front of the car catapult it forward at speed. CRAACK! the car hits the wall. The dummies crash through the windscreen. The front of the car is completely smashed in.

12.00 noon
The dummies are cut free from the wreckage. They're a little bit battered but they've survived to crash another day. They're pretty tough dummies.

1.00pm
The engineers stop for a sandwich. The dummies aren't all that hungry.

SUIT YOURSELF!

2.00 pm Telly time! The dummies have become movie stars, but they don't even know it. As the dummies are wheeled away the engineers settle themselves in front of a screen to watch an action replay of the crash on video.

You can see how Newton's First Law affects the dummies. That's the law about things continuing to move in a straight line. When the car stops, the inertia of the dummies forces

them to carry on moving – straight through the windscreen. So the force of the wall hitting the car is transferred to the poor old dummies. You can see why seat belts are lifesavers. You'd be a real dummy not to wear one.

5.00 pm The engineers set up tomorrow's test. This time the dummies will be trapped in a car as it rolls over in a crash. But that's just another smashing day in the life of the crash test dummies.
A dummy's life is full of hard knocks.

Safety first

As a result of this testing, engineers have come up with a few ingenious devices to help reduce the impact of a car crash on passengers:

SCIENTIST'S CAR

Collapsible steering wheel. If the air bag fails, the steering wheel collapses rather than spearing the driver in the chest.

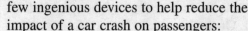

WUMPFF!

Airbags If a driver is thrown forward onto the steering wheel of most modern cars, the bag inflates for a nice soft landing.

Seat belts soak up the force that throws the body forward.

FORCE 1

Crumple zones (found in some new cars). When the car crashes, part of the front of the car is designed to crumple up and soak up some of the shock.

Side-impact bars (found in some new cars). Strengthens the doors so they won't get smashed in if another car whacks into them.

Smashing sound speeds

Fatal though they often are, the forces in a car crash are nothing compared to those in really high-speed accidents like an air crash. Or the horrible effects of falling out of an aeroplane at high speed. The effects of high speeds were studied by Austrian physicist Ernst Mach (1838–1916). Mach found that it's hard to travel faster than the speed of sound – 1,220 km per hour (760 mph). (By the way, the speed of sound is the speed sounds travel through the air.)

Here's why it's so difficult. All aircraft push air in front of them. But a plane flying at the speed of sound smashes into this air before it can escape. This makes for a violently bumpy ride that can shake the plane to pieces (not to mention your insides). In the 1940s several pilots died trying to smash the sound barrier. But in 1947 American pilot Charles E. Yeager broke the barrier in a rocket-powered plane. It was known to be dangerous to fly really, really fast, but at this time no one knew what hitting the air at these speeds would do to an unprotected body. Could it be fatal?

Fly for your life

26 February 1955, California, USA

At 9.30am precisely, ace test pilot George Franklin Smith picked up his washing. He turned left out of the launderette and walked slap bang into the worst day of his life.

He should have known better. How many people volunteer to work on a Saturday? But he had nothing better to do than finish a report. And of course when he got to work someone offered him a test flight in a gleaming brand new Super-sabre jet. This was a new type of jet plane capable of flying faster than sound.

George grinned. He loved test flying the powerful planes. In his laid-back way he replied:

YEAH, SURE I'LL TAKE HER UP. WON'T TAKE MORE THAN FORTY-FIVE MINUTES OR SO.

It wasn't worth putting on a protective suit.

As George took off he noticed the controls were a bit stiff. But there seemed nothing to worry about – the pre-flight checks had been just fine. He chatted happily to a pilot friend over the intercom.

Minutes later he broke the sound barrier. Then the plane nosed down and the controls jammed. The jet was diving to destruction at supersonic speed.

His friend's voice exploded into the headphones. "Bale out, George! Get out of there!"

As his speed increased George yelled: "Controls locked – I'm going straight down!"

He had seconds to escape or die.

About 2,100 metres below the blue sea glittered in the sunshine.

George wrenched the armrest and jettisoned the jet's perspex canopy. A tearing gale filled the cockpit. At this speed the violent force of the air pinned him down. He painfully stretched out his hand. His fingertips brushed the ejector seat handle. There was no time. No time to think of the danger. *Every* pilot who had baled out at supersonic speeds had been killed.

George's straining fingers clutched the handle. *KERBAAAM!* A powerful explosion tore him from the cockpit. He hit a wall of air. The world and the sky tumbled crazily. In a few seconds his shoes and socks, his watch and helmet were torn away. He was bleeding fast and very, very scared.

His falling body felt like a feather. "A falling body" he thought vaguely, "has no weight – it's … something to do with gravity." There was a crack and a sharp jerk as the parachute opened, its canopy trapping and slowing the air as it rushed past. Then George felt himself slip into darkness. He felt no pain as his body slammed into the sea and began to sink.

"Hey, give me a hand!" shouted the fisherman to his friend as he hauled the heavy body from the water.

The other man looked doubtful. "There's no point – I think the pilot's dead."

But George Smith was still alive. Just…

The Air Force took a month to scoop up all the mangled pieces of George's plane from the sea bed 1.6 km (1 mile) from the shore. The wreckage filled 50 barrels and still no one knew what had caused the crash.

But scientists now had a chance to study the effect of extreme forces ... on poor George's half-dead body.

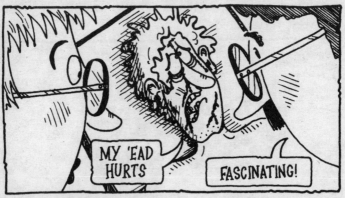

Here's what they found out:

1 As George ejected from the plane his speed boosted the effects of gravity. What we call "weight" depends on the strength of the gravity affecting our bodies. So every part of the pilot's body became 40 times heavier. You may have felt this yourself. It's that weird feeling of being stuck to your seat as you climb a roller-coaster. Only George was moving much faster so this effect was almost fatal.

2 Even his blood became heavier for a few moments. Heavy blood squirted from his heavy blood vessels. This caused a mass of bruises to appear on his body. He was so bruised that his head swelled up like a purple football.

3 George's eyelids bled after fluttering violently in the howling wind as he fell at speed.

In all George spent seven months in hospital. But he made a full recovery and went back to flying. He was the luckiest pilot in the world. Of course, every pilot's worst nightmare is to fall out of the sky. Because falling –

under the influence of gravity – can be fatal. So if you want to survive the next chapter you'd better hang on tight. And DON'T FORGET YOUR PARACHUTE!

Gruesome gravity

What goes up must come down. This old saying is true as long as you're not in outer space where things float around all the time and don't "come down". Why? Because there's no gravity in space to bring you down to Earth. So what is this unearthly force? Read on for the full and gruesome details.

Fatal forces fact file

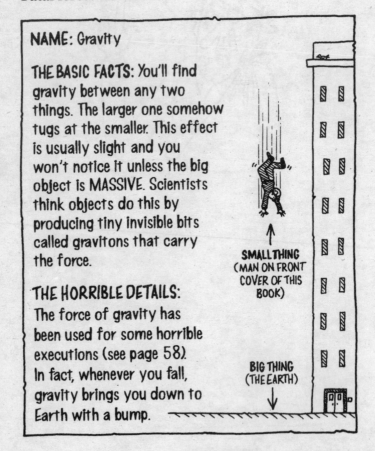

NAME: Gravity

THE BASIC FACTS: You'll find gravity between any two things. The larger one somehow tugs at the smaller. This effect is usually slight and you won't notice it unless the big object is MASSIVE. Scientists think objects do this by producing tiny invisible bits called gravitons that carry the force.

SMALL THING (MAN ON FRONT COVER OF THIS BOOK)

THE HORRIBLE DETAILS: The force of gravity has been used for some horrible executions (see page 58). In fact, whenever you fall, gravity brings you down to Earth with a bump.

BIG THING (THE EARTH)

Terminal velocity

How's this for a thrill? You go for a flight in a plane up to, say, 6,100 metres and then you jump out. And you don't use a parachute. Well – not until you've fallen halfway to the ground under the influence of gravity. Is this completely crazy? No, it's a popular sport called freefall parachuting. If you don't mind heights and enjoy a bit of danger you'll love this. If not, you'd better put on a blindfold before you read this next bit.

How to be a freefall parachutist in one quick lesson

1 Try not to look at the ground. Jump out of the plane.
2 Check your parachute is strapped securely to your back. (Come to think of it, that should have been Step One.)

3 Start tumbling. That's not something you've got to do – it's something that will happen to you anyway. You'll find your sense of balance can't help you stay upright. You'll feel sick. Try not to panic at this stage.

4 For 15 seconds you fall faster and faster. Every second you fall 9.8 metres faster until you hit – 50 metres a second (100–150 mph). That's the maximum speed you can fall. It's called terminal velocity. Gulp! It's horrible feeling there's nothing under you except empty air, but some people can't get enough of it.

WHAT DO YOU MEAN **TERMINAL** VELOCITY?

5 Good news. You won't fall any faster because the air slows you down – this force is known as drag.

6 Here's your chance to practise your freefall parachuting technique. Try to fall face downwards. Spread your arms and legs and stick your stomach out. You'll find your body curves forwards and your arms and legs are pushed backwards.

This makes a larger area for the drag to act upon. So you don't fall quite so fast. Flying squirrels and sky-diving cats do this in mid-air.

7 One minute later. Had fun? Good. You're going to hit the ground in 25 seconds. Better pull your parachute rip cord now or you'll really fall foul of gravity. And make a rather deep hole in the ground.

8 As you land make sure you drop down to a squatting position. Bending your knees soaks up some force as you hit the ground. Enjoyed it? Great – you'll be falling over yourself to make another jump.

More gruesome gravity

In the past gravity was used to make executions more efficient. During a hanging the victim dropped through a trapdoor and gravity acting on the rope broke the victim's neck. If the drop was too far the force yanked their head off too. Gruesome!

Another gruesome method of execution was the guillotine. This featured a 30.4 kg weight attached to a sharp blade. The force powering the gruesome blade as it fell was gravity. In the 1790s working model guillotines were popular children's toys. Their parents must have been off their heads.

In England in the seventeenth century criminals who refused to plead guilty or not guilty at their trials were crushed to death under heavy weights. Once again it was gravity doing the damage. You may be interested to know that a louse can withstand a force of 500,000 times its own weight. Unfortunately for the criminals, humans scrunch more easily.

Now for something a bit less fatal. Hopefully. You'd think that lying on a bed of nails would turn you into a gruesome human pin cushion. Surely gravity pins you to those nasty nails? Not necessarily. You can press down with a force of 450 g on a nail without harm. (Don't try proving this at home – nails are usually crawling with disgusting germs.) So 400 nails can support a huge 182 kg man for a comfortable night's sleep. Bet that's a weight off your mind.

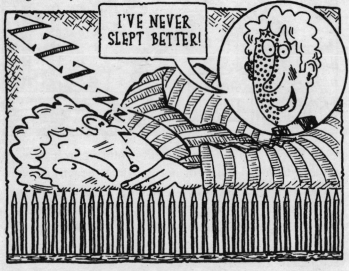

Fatal expressions

Answer:

No. He's got a weight problem. Scientists say "mass" instead of weight because weight is just a measure of how strongly gravity is pulling you towards the Earth. Also scientists measure mass in a unit called the "slug". The overweight scientist in the picture weighs ten slugs (146 kg). He should cut out chocolate and sticky puddings, or move to the moon. The moon's gravity is weaker than Earth's, so a human only weighs $\frac{1}{6}$ as much there.

Test your teacher

Your teacher's bound to fall down on this really tricky question. Smile sweetly and say:

EXCUSE ME, IS IT TRUE THAT GRAVITY CAN HELP YOU LOSE WEIGHT?

Answer:

Yes – but you'd have to be in a lift with a set of scales to prove it. If one day the lift cable snaps, quickly leap on the scales. In the few seconds you take to hurtle to the ground you're weightless! Weight is just a measure of gravity's pull. But when you fall you're not resisting gravity and you're weightless! You can blame Galileo for all this, he was the first person to discover how the force works.

61

Hall of fame: Galileo Galilei (1564–1642)
Nationality: Italian

Young Galileo wanted to study maths (strange boy), but his dad forced him to learn medicine instead. Doctors got more pay than mathematicians. But sneaky Galileo secretly studied sums until his dad gave up on him. When he was 25, Galileo became a maths professor at Pisa University. Then he got interested in gravity and performed amazing experiments to measure the force. Here's what his notebooks may have looked like.

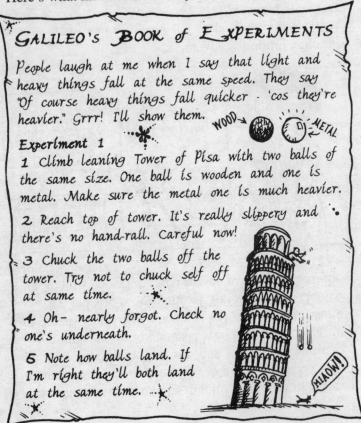

GALILEO'S BOOK of EXPERIMENTS

People laugh at me when I say that light and heavy things fall at the same speed. They say "Of course heavy things fall quicker - 'cos they're heavier." Grrr! I'll show them.

WOOD → ○ ○ ← METAL

Experiment 1

1 Climb leaning Tower of Pisa with two balls of the same size. One ball is wooden and one is metal. Make sure the metal one is much heavier.

2 Reach top of tower. It's really slippery and there's no hand-rail. Careful now!

3 Chuck the two balls off the tower. Try not to chuck self off at same time.

4 Oh - nearly forgot. Check no one's underneath.

5 Note how balls land. If I'm right they'll both land at the same time.

MIAOW!

ME

People still don't believe me.
Huh - this'll teach them a lesson.

Experiment 2

1 Get a wooden board with a little wooden gully on it. Line it with some nice shiny parchment made from animal skin with the fat scraped off.

USE SKIN FROM CAT KILLED IN EXPERIMENT 1

2 Raise the gully on a slope and roll a bronze ball down it. (If you don't have a bronze ball any other metal will do.)

3 Be sure to precisely measure the time taken for the ball to roll to the bottom of the slope. OOPS - silly me, I was about to forget, no one's invented an accurate clock yet. Better use pulse to time ball's speed. Mustn't get too excited, or my pulse will be racing. Better repeat the test a few times to make sure.

3, 4, 5, 6, 7...

RUMBLE RUMBLE

4 I believe gravity makes things accelerate at the same speed. If I'm right balls of different weights will roll at the same speed too.

Notes:

1 Galileo was proved right in both experiments.

2 It should be pointed out that boring old historians reckon there's no proof Galileo performed the first experiment. Huh – why spoil a good story?

Galileo's genius

There's no doubt Galileo was a genius. He invented the thermometer, a pendulum driven clock and an amazing compass that you could use to work out the purity of metals. He even discovered that cannonballs fall in a curved path. They move forwards at a constant speed and downwards at an increasing speed under the influence of gravity. This fatal discovery helped gunners fire more accurately and kill more people.

Could you think like Galileo? Now's your chance to find out.

Burning ambition quiz

1 You are Galileo. You look through the newly invented telescope and see planets orbiting the sun. (As Newton later proved, gravity stops them wandering off into space.) But there's one teeny-little problem. Important people in the Church claim planets go round the Earth. They're all-powerful in Italy. And they don't want a smarty-pants scientist proving them wrong. You realize you'd be wise to get the backing of these people. What do you do?

a) Start a reasoned debate.
b) Get them to look through your telescope.
c) Shout at them until they admit you're right.

LISTEN, YOU OLD FOOL, THE POTATO GOES ROUND THE BOILED EGG – NOT THE OTHER WAY ROUND!

2 You reckon the Church's experts that you talked to are friendly. They aren't. Your enemies falsely accuse you of being anti-Church. What do you do?
a) Go into hiding.
b) Write a book making fun of your enemies.
c) Set the record straight in a public statement.

3 In 1623 you have a stroke of luck. An old pal of yours is elected Pope. You drop in for a chat. He allows you to write a book so long as it doesn't support your views. What's in the book?
a) Support for your views and amusing abuse of your enemies.
b) A balanced survey of the different opinions which doesn't come to any conclusion.
c) A cleverly written argument which seems to back the traditional view whilst actually making it look stupid.
4 Your book is a best-seller but the Pope is chewing the carpet. You're accused of heresy and put on trial before

the dreaded Inquisition. Your enemies forge a letter that claims the Church had banned you from teaching your views. If you're found guilty you could be tied to a stake and burnt alive. What do you do?

a) Proudly insist you were right.

b) Quietly remind the Pope that you're his friend.

c) Crack a joke about liking your "stake" well done.

5 In a bid to scare you, the Inquisition show you the torture chamber that is used to extract confessions. You see the rack, the thumbscrews and the red hot pincers. What do you say?

a) OK, where's the confession – I'll sign anything... Oh dear, I can't sign that, it's not grovelling enough.

b) The truth is the truth. I scorn your puny instruments of torture and laugh in the face of danger.

c) Can I have 20 years to think about it, please?

Wobbly balance
Everything has a centre of gravity. Imagine a tightrope walker.

Answers:

1 b) Galileo talked to leading Church astronomers. They looked through the telescope and saw he was right. But they refused to admit it.

2 b) This was silly, because Galileo had been ordered not to talk about his views.

3 c) Galileo's book is a chat between three people. The person who backs his view is smart but the person who backs the Church's view is called "Simplicius". Can you guess why?

4 a) Of course, Galileo was right, but the Church wouldn't admit it until 1922. Galileo would have been 100 per cent delighted if he hadn't been 100 per cent dead by then. Fortunately, even in Galileo's own century, scientists in other countries, such as Isaac Newton, read his books. The scientists used Galileo's discoveries as a starting point to find out more about gravity and how the planets moved.

5 a) OK, Galileo didn't say this, but he did confess to the Inquisition that he was wrong. Don't blame him. Galileo spent the rest of his life at home under arrest. He continued to study forces but he never touched a telescope again. It was too dangerous. And now for something even more dangerous…

Her centre of balance is the point inside her body where gravity is pulling most strongly. If this crucial point is supported underneath and the performer's weight is evenly balanced around it she's OK. If not there'll be a gloopy mess on the pavement. Yet some balancing acts seem impossible.

Wobbly balancing quiz

See if you can guess which of these incredible balancing acts are true and which are false.

1 In 1553 a Dutch acrobat balanced on one foot on the weathervane of St Paul's Cathedral, London waving a 4.6 metre (15 foot) streamer. And he didn't fall off. TRUE/FALSE

2 In 1859 French tightrope walker Jean Blondin (1824–1897) walked across the raging Niagara Falls 50 metres in the air. And he was wearing a blindfold. TRUE/FALSE

3 In 1773 Dutch acrobat Leopold van Trump juggled ten tomatoes whilst balancing on a tightrope 30 metres in the air. If he had fallen he might have invented tomato ketchup. TRUE/FALSE

4 In 1842 a Miss Cooke wowed London circus goers when she sat at a table and drank a glass of wine. Boring? Not really. Everything was balanced on a high wire. TRUE/FALSE

5 In 1995 Aleksandr Bendikov of Belarus balanced a pyramid made of 880 coins. The coin pyramid was upside down and balanced on top of the edge of a single coin. Luckily, no one needed change for the bus. TRUE/FALSE

6 In 1996 American Bryan Berg built a house of cards 100 storeys high – that's 5.85 metres TRUE/FALSE

ATISHOO!

BLAST YOU! I MEAN BLESS YOU

7 In 1990 Brazilian Leandro Henrique Basseto cycled on one wheel of his bicycle for 100 minutes. TRUE/FALSE

Answers:

1 TRUE. Some people will do *anything* to get attention.

2 TRUE. Blondin also went across on stilts. By then he was just showing off.

3 FALSE

4 TRUE

5 TRUE

6 TRUE He built the record house of cards in Copenhagen, Denmark. Couldn't he find anything more exciting to do?

7 FALSE. In fact he cycled for an incredible 640 minutes.

69

Yes, it's amazing what incredible death-defying, gravity-defying, balancing acts people can do just as long as the force of gravity is exactly balanced. But getting it right on the high-wire certainly puts you under pressure. And oddly enough, the next chapter is about pressure too. The kind of pressure that can fatally crush a human being. Ouch!

I'VE BEEN UNDER A LOT OF PRESSURE RECENTLY

UNDER pressure

Air and water are common enough on Earth but they are vital chemicals – in fact we couldn't live without them. But if they're under pressure it's hard to live with them. And they can easily prove fatal.

Fatal forces fact file

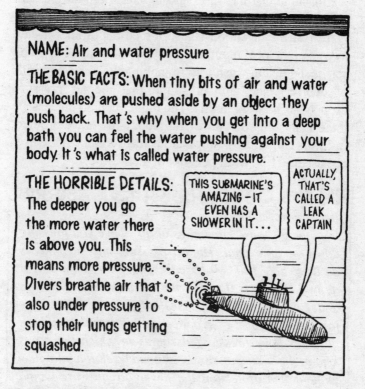

NAME: Air and water pressure

THE BASIC FACTS: When tiny bits of air and water (molecules) are pushed aside by an object they push back. That's why when you get into a deep bath you can feel the water pushing against your body. It's what is called water pressure.

THE HORRIBLE DETAILS: The deeper you go the more water there is above you. This means more pressure. Divers breathe air that's also under pressure to stop their lungs getting squashed.

THIS SUBMARINE'S AMAZING – IT EVEN HAS A SHOWER IN IT...

ACTUALLY, THAT'S CALLED A LEAK CAPTAIN

One of the first people to study air pressure was French physicist Blaise Pascal.

Hall of fame: Blaise Pascal (1623–1662)
Nationality: French

Blaise Pascal had no sense of humour. Not surprising really, he suffered all his life from violent indigestion so he didn't have the stomach for too many jokes. But that didn't stop brainy Blaise from making some amazing discoveries. At the age of 19 he built a machine to help his tax collector dad count up the loot. And in 1646 he invented a barometer – a machine that measures air pressure. High air pressure pushes a column of mercury upwards.

To test his invention Blaise forced his brother-in-law to walk up a local mountain carrying the barometer. (The scientist's health wasn't up to making the climb himself, of course.) The climber found that the air pressure dropped as he went higher. The higher you go the less air there is pushing down on you. Today the brave brother-in-law is forgotten but pressure is measured in "Pascals". (1 Pascal = 1 Newton per square metre.)

Bet you never knew!

Imagine all those kilometres of air above you pressing down on your head. The air pressure on your body is an incredible 100,000 Pascals. That's the same weight as two elephants. Luckily, the air inside your body is under pressure too. It pushes outwards with the same force so you don't even notice it. Planes that fly at high altitudes have pressurized cabins in which the air is kept at the same pressure as ground level. If a pilot flew without this protection the lower air pressure would cause air bubbles in his or her body to get bigger. The guts and lungs would swell painfully and air bubbles trapped in fillings could make their teeth explode.

Dare you discover … how air pressure helps you drink?

What you need:

Yourself

A bottle of your favourite drink (it's all in the interests of science) – just so long as the bottle's got a narrow neck.

What you do:

1 Try drinking from the bottle. Sit upright and tip the bottle up so it's level with your mouth. You can easily suck the liquid up.

2 Now stick the mouth of the bottle in your mouth. Wrap your lips around the neck of the bottle. Now try to drink. What do you notice?

a) It's as easy as before.

b) You can't suck any more drink up.

c) You dribble uncontrollably into your drink.

73

Terrible teacher joke

Under pressure

1 The first man-made vacuum was made by Otto von Guericke (1602–1686) Mayor of Magdeburg, Germany. In his spare time Otto was keen on scientific experiments but in 1631 Magdeburg was destroyed in war and 70,000 people were killed. Von Guericke got away and carried on researching.

2 In 1647 he tried pumping air from a beer cask. But more air got in and made a strange whistling noise.

3 So he put the beer cask in a barrel of water. Water was sucked into the cask with a strange squelching noise.

4 Next he made a hollow copper ball. But when he pumped the air out it was crushed by an unseen force.

5 In 1654 von Guericke made a hollow ball from two stronger copper cups and pumped out the air. He'd made a vacuum. The pressure of the air outside jammed the cups together. It was this pressure that had crushed the earlier ball.

6 Fifty men couldn't pull the cups apart.

7 Two teams of horses didn't stand a chance.

8 But when von Guericke pumped air into the hollow centre the cups fell apart.

Some pressing facts

1 In the 1890s Aimée, a young circus performer, used the power of vacuums to walk upside down. Her shoes had suction caps attached to them and as she walked the air was pushed out of the caps. The pressure of the air outside the caps then glued her feet to a board hung from the ceiling. Very im-press-ive!

2 Champagne in a bottle is under pressure too. This is due to all the gas bubbles squeezed into the drink. When shaken and heated the cork fires at 12.3 metres a second – as fast as a rock blasted with dynamite. It definitely makes a party go with a bang.

3 Pressurized liquid or gases are used in hydraulic machines such as the powerful pistons that lift crane jibs. One early hydraulic machine was a nineteenth-century vacuum cleaner. Water was squirted one way and the falling pressure sucked in air and dirt behind it. But when water went the wrong way it flooded your home.

I THINK WE'LL STICK TO THE DUSTPAN AND BRUSH, POLLY

4 In 1868 American inventor George Westinghouse (1846–1914) made an air brake. It used the cushioning effect of air pressure to halt a train. Rail tycoon Cornelius Vanderbilt called it a "foolish notion". He didn't think air could stop a train. But nowadays air brakes are used on buses and lorries too.

Air pressure can do amazing things but could it also haul a train? It took a genius to see the possibilities in this "train of thought". A hard-driving ruthless workaholic genius in a black top hat.

Hall of fame: Isambard Kingdom Brunel
(1806–1859) Nationality: British

Isambard Kingdom Brunel dedicated his life to engineering. He developed some spectacular engineering projects that used the forces of nature to help make people's lives easier. He built railways, giant iron ships and tunnels on a grand scale. At times he was so wrapped up in his work that he showed little concern for others. He even sent his crippled son to a school where there were daily floggings. When the child complained bossy Brunel snapped at him:

Issie loved to attempt the seemingly impossible. Sometimes he was successful but he also made many fatal mistakes. This story is about one of them ... a railway powered by air pressure.

Pipe dreams

Devon, England 1848

Isambard Kingdom Brunel chewed on his giant-sized cigar as he strode angrily along the railway. As usual his mind was jumping with ideas. Fantastic ideas. Mighty plans. Pipe dreams. They had all seemed so easy. Once.

Four years ago Brunel and some other leading engineers visited Ireland to see the world's first "atmospheric railway". A railway where the carriages were pulled quickly and silently. Pulled along by the amazing power of air.

The idea was simple...

How to build your own atmospheric railway.

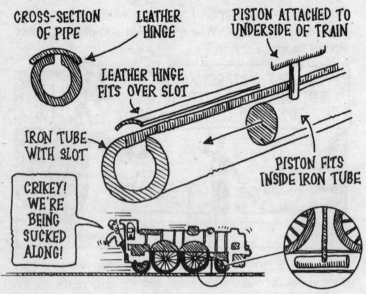

CROSS-SECTION
OF PIPE

LEATHER
HINGE

PISTON ATTACHED TO
UNDERSIDE OF TRAIN

LEATHER HINGE
FITS OVER SLOT

IRON TUBE
WITH SLOT

PISTON FITS
INSIDE IRON TUBE

CRIKEY!
WE'RE
BEING
SUCKED
ALONG!

And here's how it worked.

1 Powerful steam engines pump the air from the pipe.

2 A piston travels along the pipe. It's pushed by air trying to rush back into the vacuum.

3 The piston is linked to passenger carriages and provides the moving power.

The other engineers laughed at the strangely silent railway. They thought it was impractical. But Isambard was quietly impressed. He suggested using atmospheric pressure for the South Devon Railway. But he forgot to mention to anyone that the Irish railway was always breaking down. Little old ladies rushed to sink their savings in a scheme backed by the world's greatest engineer. But the pipe dream soon turned into a pipe nightmare.

Now Brunel had come to see things for himself and young Tom the signalman's boy was showing him around.

"It's the leather hinges, Mr Brunel," said Tom slightly in awe of the great man. "They dry and crack in cold winter weather. And they rot in warm sunshine."

"So I see," said Brunel wrinkling his nose in distaste. "What's that appalling smell?"

"That'll be the fish oil. The railway pays people to walk along the line and paint the leather with soap and fish liver oil to keep it soft. Smells disgusting, it does."

They walked on until they reached one of the massive brick-built pumping sheds.

"Here's the other problem!" cried Tom. He nervously twisted his pale sweaty fingers. "It's the pipes…"

"What do you mean pipes?" bellowed Brunel above the noise of the engines. The huge steam engine snorted foul black smoke like an angry dragon. The gasping pumps sucked the air from the hollow iron pipes. And with the air came a stream of horrible things.

Oily water, rust and dead rats.

Rats. *Water.*

"How did they get there?" Brunel roared into the boy's ear. But he'd already guessed the terrible truth.

Hungry rats chewed the oily leather flaps until they were no longer air-tight. Water seeped in and rusted the pipes.

The famous engineer strode on furiously with the signalman's boy jogging to keep up. Suddenly Brunel bent down to touch the rat nibbled leather. Tom watched in fascinated horror. "No!" he shouted.

Brunel had his hand on the flap when Tom grabbed his arm.

"Stand aside boy!" ordered Brunel curtly.

"*Please* don't touch it," gasped Tom.

"Why NOT?"

Then Brunel saw the ghastly danger.

The vacuum inside the pipe wasn't 100 per cent. But it could still pluck his finger bones from their sockets. Scrunch, squelch, plop. No more fingers.

He backed off, muttering. There were some things even the great Brunel dared not do.

In February 1848 Brunel told the Company the problems were almost solved. But seven months later he advised the directors to scrap the entire project. The little old ladies had lost their savings. And they were angry.

So how did Brunel make it up to them?

a) He offered to build a new railway for nothing.

b) He said he wouldn't send his bill for engineering advice.

c) He offered them a lifetime's supply of smelly fish oil.

Answer:

b) Brunel kindly offered not to send his bill. Not just yet. Bet that cheered them up. There was a lot of anger and friction. You get friction in the world of forces too. But this sort of friction can wreck machines and spark fatal fires. That's why the next chapter is *RED HOT*.

I'LL GIVE YOU FRICTION!

FACTS ABOUT FRICTION

Newton said that a moving object would carry on moving for ever if another force didn't slow it down. That force is called friction. People use the word friction to mean aggro, anger or annoyance. Like a really bad day at school. And in the world of fatal forces friction can also often spoil your whole day.

Fatal forces fact file

NAME: Friction

THE BASIC FACTS: You get friction when two moving objects brush together. Tiny bumps on each side stick together. They make heat and sound as the energy of moving objects turns into heat and sound energy.

THE HORRIBLE DETAILS: Friction causes problems for machines because it slows them down or makes them overheat. But lack of friction also causes fatal problems. If your bike brake blocks get worn they can't grip the wheels with enough friction. So you can't stop. Help!

SQUEEZE

SQUEEZE

Mind you, the man who discovered friction had an amazing life-story. He could almost have been a character from friction – er, fiction.

Hall of fame: Benjamin Thompson (Count Rumford of Bavaria) (1753–1814) Nationality: American

Ben Thompson was a teacher who escaped from school. He was born in the United States and besides being a teacher, he was a gymnast and a medical student. Until the war. The American colonists were fighting for their independence from Britain. But which side should Ben choose? The Americans or the British?

Rumour has it that he chose both. He spied for the British *and* the Americans. He was a sort of a double-agent. But the British never knew this and King George III gave Ben a knighthood when the war was over.

But Ben liked the excitement of being at war. He said he didn't want to "vegetate in England". So what did he do? Simple! He went to Bavaria as a special adviser on War to the government and became Minister for War in 1793.

As Minister of War, Ben devised a cunning plan. The streets were full of beggars and the army was short of uniforms. Ben's idea was to force the beggars to make uniforms. But how should he feed the beggars? After much research Ben found the cheapest food was watery vegetable soup. So he "vegetated" in Bavaria instead of in England – ha, ha. Ben was so keen on his idea he even published a book of recipes. Could this be a new line in school dinners? Then he had a second brainwave.

He put soldiers to work growing potatoes to make the soup to feed the beggars who made their uniforms. Ben's plan was a great success so at least it didn't land him in the soup! Brainy Ben made many other interesting discoveries. A new chimney for houses, a new stove and a coffee percolator to put on the stove.

And then he discovered friction.

One day Ben was watching a cannon being made. The barrel of the cannon was bored by a drill. Ben could feel the heat wafting off the cannon. In those days people thought heat was an invisible liquid. But Ben found you got extra heat if you used a blunt drill. So he figured the heat was produced by the drill. Dead right. The blunt drill had tiny bumps on its surface – and this caused extra friction. And more heat.

Fact or friction?

Often, just like Benjamin Thompson, physicists draw conclusions from things they noticed. Could you do this? Here are some everyday happenings. Which ones are caused by friction?

1 Friction helps you to build a house of cards.

2 Friction explains how you can whip a table cloth off a fully-laid table without breaking anything.

3 Friction makes electrical equipment heat up.

4 The patterns on tyres causes friction with the road. This helps to control the vehicle.

5 People use friction to start fires.

6 Friction helps skiers to ski up hills.

7 Runners use friction to run without slipping.

8 Friction causes people to get burnt by snow.

Answers:

1 Fact. Tiny bumps on the surface of the cards help them to stick to the surface of the table. That's friction. It works if the cards are at a steep angle.

2 Friction. The inertia of the crockery and the force of gravity pins it to the table. If you pull the table cloth fast enough there isn't enough friction to pull the crockery off the table. However, practising this trick at home may cause fatal friction with your family.

3 Fact. As the electrical current runs through the circuits it causes friction which heats up the machine. That's why TV's can burst into flames if you cover their ventilation holes.

4 Friction. Smooth tyres provide more friction in dry weather. The treads are better in wet weather. The wheel scoops the water out of the way so the tyres can grip the road.

5 Fact. One of your ancestors hit on a hot method of lighting fires. Rub two sticks together. The heat of the friction can set fire to some dried fungus. Later on people found that partially burnt underwear caught fire again very easily. So it was ideal for getting a blaze going.

6 Fact. Traditional up-hill skis used sealskin for this purpose. Nowadays they have man-made bristles. It's kinder to seals.

7 Fact. Spiked shoes increase friction with the track.

8 Fact. Crazy skiers can suffer serious burns if they go too fast and then fall over. At high speeds, friction causes enough heat to burn the skin before the snow melts.

Messed-up machines

Here's the bad news about friction. It slows machines down. Yes, it's a real spanner in the works for generations of freaky physicists who've tried to devise the ultimate machine. One that keeps on working without power. Perpetual motion.

Between 1617 and 1906 the British Patent Office received ideas for 600 perpetual motion machines. None worked.

Here are four more. Which one was successful?

1 A perpetual bicycle

The power for this bike comes from your bum bouncing on the saddle. This drives the rear wheel using a drive belt. So you could cycle for ever or until you get a sore bum.

2 A self-powered pump

The water-lifting pump is powered by a waterwheel that is powered by falling water.

3 A perpetual motion clock

Changes in atmospheric pressure shift the glass bulb up or down and this powers a ratchet that winds the clock up.

4 A perpetual wind machine

Dreamt up by an Italian doctor in 1500. Air from the fan is funnelled down a horn linked to a propeller which in turn powers the fan.

A hot halt

Perpetual motion, unfortunately, breaks a law of physics. The Second Law of Thermodynamics to be exact. (Thermodynamics is the branch of physics to do with heat and energy. It's a subject you can really warm to.) The Second Law of Thermodynamics says that energy is lost from a machine as sound, noise, heat and, of course, friction.

So the machine stops because it runs out of energy. By the way, the First Law of Thermodynamics says you can turn energy from motion into heat. And it's true. Try rubbing your hands and friction turns the energy of your moving hands into a nice warm sensation.

A slippery subject

Sometimes we want friction. Brakes, tyres, rubber-soled shoes, sandpaper and driving belts in machines would be useless without it.

THESE 'FRICTION' BOOTS ARE GREAT FOR WALKING UP STEEP HILLS!

But sometimes we don't want friction. We want things to go smoothly. That's why some slippery character invented lubrication. A lubricant such as oil fills out the little bumps that cause friction and allows the surfaces to slide past one another.

Most winter sports depend on lubrication. Sledges, skis and skates move easily because they melt a thin layer of ice beneath them. So they float along on this watery lubricant without too much friction. Until you slip over.

VERY LITTLE FRICTION

LOTS OF FRICTION

Lubrication also launches ships. That's why in the Middle Ages slipways were coated in revoltingly greasy animal fat. A slave got the risky job of knocking away the props under the ship. At the last minute the slave had to jump clear. If he slipped the ship would crush him – that's why they called it the slip-way. If the slave survived he was given his freedom.

But if lubrication is lethal, friction can be fatal. That was certainly the case in Rome four centuries ago.

Fatal friction
Rome, 1586

It was an ancient obelisk. For 2,000 years it had lain forgotten in the dirt, west of St Peter's Cathedral. But times had changed. The Pope decided that the stone would look great in front of St Peter's. But how could it be raised? It was quite a problem. The obelisk weighed 327 tonnes.

"They say," murmured old Roberto, "that two engineers turned down the job. Reckoned it couldn't be done."

"I can see why," replied young Marco gazing in awe at the huge stone in its protective cage.

"Well – we'd better give it a try. Gotta earn our pay," grumbled Roberto with a wheezy cough. He and Marco were amongst hundreds of sailors hired to raise the obelisk. They took up their ropes.

The square was ringed by crowds. Thousands of people were cheering and waving handkerchiefs and waiting impatiently for the big event. A smartly dressed young man leapt onto a platform.

Roberto screwed up his creased old face in a scowl. "That's Fontana – he's the engineer who claims he can do it. What a big-head!"

"People of Rome!" proclaimed the young man. "Today we'll raise this great monument from the past. When the trumpet sounds you sailors must pull the ropes. Only stop when you hear the bell. It's vital that these signals are obeyed in silence. There must be no talking on pain of death!" The young man pointed sternly to the nearby gallows.

There was a shocked silence.

The older sailor made the sign of the cross. "That's a bit over the top," he whispered.

The sailors spat on their hands. The moist spit would stop friction with the rope burning the skin off their fingers.

The trumpet blared. The harsh note echoed around the square. Silently the men took the strain. The ropes creaked. Windlasses squealed. Capstans groaned round. Slowly, painfully the great stone began to lift.

Then the bell rang. Everyone rested for a few moments. The trumpet sounded again. Once again the sailors' muscles bunched and knotted until sweat trickled down their backs. Then disaster struck.

The ropes jammed – halted by friction between the ropes and windlasses. The sailors pulled the ropes until their faces screwed up in agony. Nothing moved. The taut ropes groaned and frayed. The stone tottered. Young Marco saw the danger. He shouted instantly: "Water, give water to the ropes!" Then he realized what he'd done. And knew he must die.

"Seize him!" screamed Fontana, his voice cracking with tension and disappointment. "Seize him for breaking the silence!"

Strong arms grabbed Marco. The guards dragged the young sailor towards the scaffold and the waiting executioner. The people gasped in horror but no one dared speak.

"I'm sorry," whispered Marco. But it was too late.

The executioner tightened the harsh hemp rope around Marco's bare throat.

A thin, old priest touched the sailor's arm.

"What's your last request?" the priest mumbled.

"Please, father," croaked Marco. His heart was racing and he couldn't speak clearly. His throat was dry and the rope didn't help. "Please, tell them to pour water on the ropes."

"I don't know if that's possible, my son."

"*Please* do it!"

The steel-helmeted guards beat their drums. It was the signal for the execution to begin.

The priest hurried over to Fontana. The young engineer nodded his head impatiently. A large water pitcher was found and its contents poured over the straining ropes.

"Come on mate, let's get it over with," said the executioner cheerfully shoving Marco up the ladder of death.

Just then a trumpet blared and the ropes took the strain.

"Why were the people cheering?" thought Marco wildly. Were they pleased to see him die?

No. The ropes were moving easily. The stone was being lifted smoothly and quickly. At the foot of the ladder stood Domenico Fontana. Shamefaced.

"Release that man!" he shouted.

As a sailor Marco was used to hauling wet ropes at sea. He knew that there was less friction on wet ropes because the water acted as a lubricant. You'll be pleased to know that the brave sailor was pardoned and given his freedom. But what was his reward for saving the obelisk?

a) A golden pitcher of water.

b) Tea with the Pope.

c) His very own ship.

Well, hopefully you won't slip-up over this easy experiment.

Dare you discover … how to give things the slip?

What you need:

BANANA

COOKING OIL

PLASTIC BOTTLE TOP

KITCHEN TOWELS

TWO PLASTIC FOOD TRAYS

What you do:

1 Flick the bottle top along the first tray. Make sure the top stays on the tray and doesn't fly through the air.

2 Carefully pour a few drops of cooking oil on the first tray. Smear it over the surface with a kitchen towel until the surface is shiny and there is no extra oil on the tray.

3 Now flick the bottle top again as hard as before. Note what happens.

4 Mash up the banana and, using another kitchen towel, smear a little of the mixture over the second tray. Make sure the surface is smooth and shiny and there are no lumps of banana left.

5 *(optional)* Mash the remaining banana with a little cream and sugar. Eat it. Tell your feeble-minded folks it's all part of the experiment. Who said science was tough?

6 Now flick the bottle top again as hard as before.

What do you notice?

a) Both the oil and the banana make good lubricants. They help the top move faster.

b) The top stuck to the banana and skimmed along over the oil.

c) The top stuck in the oil but skimmed over the banana.

Answer:

a) Lubricating oils are squeezed from peanuts, coconuts or bits of dead fish. In some countries bananas are used because they're slippery too. That's why you slip on a banana skin!

HORRIBLE HEALTH WARNING!

Please do not test your lubricants in any of the following places:

1. School corridors – they're slippery enough already.

PATIENCE BEING STRETCHED

2. Your teacher's chair.

3. Stairs. They could prove your downfall!

SCHOOL TIE BEING STRETCHED

Any of these things could stretch a grown-up's patience to breaking point. But you ain't seen nothing yet. The next chapter's really taking the strain.

Stretching and straining

Hold an elastic band between your fingers. Pull one end ever so carefully. The elastic band is storing the energy you put into pulling it. Let go – the released energy sends the elastic band flying. Oh dear – why does a teacher always get in the way? But just tell him that it's all part of a very technical scientific experiment – he'll understand! One of the first people to experiment with stretching was scientist Robert Hooke.

Hall of fame: Robert Hooke (1635–1703)
Nationality: British

After his bust-ups with Newton (see page 24), Robert must have known all about tension. But this talented scientist was interested in everything from telescopes to making flying machines that didn't fly. Incredibly, he also worked as an architect, an astronomer, a mechanic and a model maker. Yes. Hooke liked working at full-stretch.

According to one story Robert wrote a strange code in his will which deciphered into Latin reads "*ut tensio sic vis*". Mean anything to you? Thought not. Further translated into English it means "as the extension so the force". And these weird words turned out to be Hooke's Law on stretching. Imagine hanging a weight on a spring – the spring stretches. Double the weight and the spring stretches twice as far. Simple, innit?

Dare you discover 1 ... what happens when something stretches?

What you need:
Yourself
A 0.5-cm-thick elastic band

What you do:
Suddenly stretch the elastic band.
Put it against your face.
What happens and why?

a) The elastic band feels strangely cold because all the energy has been stretched out of it.

b) The elastic band feels warm. This is due to the energy that you have provided by stretching it.

c) The elastic band feels warm because stretching causes friction with your hot sweaty little fingers.

Answer:
b) The band briefly stores energy from the force that stretches it. The energy tries to escape as heat and that's why the band feels hot.

Dare you discover 2 … the power of an elastic band?
Here's a machine that uses stored energy in an elastic band to get moving. Ask an adult to help with some of the cutting.

What you need:

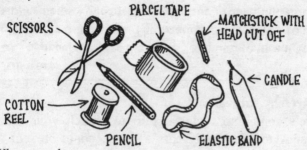

SCISSORS

PARCEL TAPE

MATCHSTICK WITH HEAD CUT OFF

CANDLE

COTTON REEL

PENCIL

ELASTIC BAND

What you do:

1 Cut 2.5 cm off the bottom of the candle.

2 Remove the wick from the wax and make its middle hole large enough for the elastic band.

3 Pass the elastic band through the centres of the candle stump and the cotton reel.

4 Pass the matchstick through the elastic band at its cotton reel end. Secure the matchstick with a strip of parcel tape.

5 Pass the pencil through the elastic band at its candle end.

6 Wind the elastic band by turning the pencil. Watch your vehicle creep along as the elastic band unwinds. Compare its performance on rough and smooth slopes. What do you notice?

a) It climbs better on smooth slopes.
b) It climbs better on rough slopes.
c) It can't climb slopes.

A stretchy subject

Here's some more elastic info to stretch your brain cells. A few hundred years ago you could be sent to prison in England for a long stretch. Stretched out on a timber frame with rollers at each end. This was the rack. The most anyone was ever stretched on a rack was 15 cm. After that their arm and leg joints popped out of their sockets. Rumours that racks were used in schools are just "tall stories". No – teachers just racked children's *brains*.

100

In the 1700s rubber thread was used in clothes and underwear. Sadly, the rubber melted in hot weather and cracked in cold.

In 1839 scientists discovered a chemical treatment that stopped this happening and rubber thread known as elastic was used in corsets and knickers from the 1930s. (Corsets are the tight-fitting garments some women wore to squeeze their bulging bodies into shape. Before elastic, corsets were reinforced with bits of whale bone.)

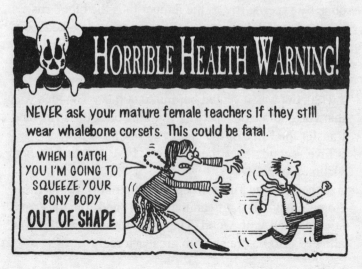

HORRIBLE HEALTH WARNING!

NEVER ask your mature female teachers if they still wear whalebone corsets. This could be fatal.

WHEN I CATCH YOU I'M GOING TO SQUEEZE YOUR BONY BODY **OUT OF SHAPE**

Nowadays man-made elastic is used for much more than just corsets – including the rope bungee jumpers use. Would you want to bungee jump?

If your answer to this question is "ARGGGGGH!" you wouldn't envy Gregory Riffi who in 1992 jumped 249.9 metres from a helicopter over France. With his life hanging by a thread – all right – an elastic rope.

By the way, bungee jumping isn't usually fatal if it's done by experts. But as the jumper falls the blood rushes to their head and this can make their eyeballs bleed a bit. Another sport that depends on stretching is archery.

Big bad bows
1 The bow was invented before 20,000 BC. The idea was that you could store energy by pulling back the string and transfer the force of the energy to fire the arrow.
2 Five seconds later the bow may have claimed its first victim. Ooops!
3 In the 900s the Turks hit upon a better bow. It was made from grisly bits of animal horn and tendons and strengthened with wood. The outward curve of the bow allowed it to be drawn with greater force.

4 Meanwhile the Europeans had invented the crossbow. This deadly weapon could fire a bolt 305 metres

5 But the crossbow string had to be cranked slowly back. And during that time ordinary archers with ordinary bows were so skilled, they could turn the crossbow soldier into a pin-cushion in no time – unless he bolted first.

6 And then a Welsh person invented the long-bow. It could fire an arrow 320 metres. And straight through chain mail. At shorter ranges, the arrows could pierce armour too.

CROSS BOWMAN

GRRRR

CROSSBOW

7 Modern bows are really high-tech.

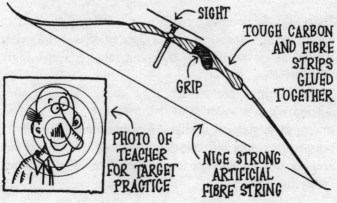

SIGHT

TOUGH CARBON AND FIBRE STRIPS GLUED TOGETHER

GRIP

PHOTO OF TEACHER FOR TARGET PRACTICE

NICE STRONG ARTIFICIAL FIBRE STRING

8 In free-style shooting the archers lie on their back, strap the bow to their feet and draw the string with both hands. Of course, it isn't only stretchy things that can store force. Springs can do this too when you push them down and then they pop up again. You'll be surprised to know that the earliest springs were used 600 years ago in mousetraps. And springs can spring real surprises on you. Here are seven more.

Seven springy surprises

1 The first toasters sold in 1919 had powerful springs that shot toast into the air. Bet that surprised a few people.

2 Springs sometimes break. Metal fatigue does for a cheap spring after about 100,000 extensions, but a better spring lasts over 10,000,000 extensions. A surprisingly long stretch.

3 Bed springs are a surprising shape. They're cone shaped – that's wider at their top than at the base. This makes them squeeze easily at first but the harder they're pressed the more difficult they are to squash. A bed that feels comfy and springy to you feels like a rock to a big, sprawling grown-up.

4 You know the circus act where a person is fired from a cannon? You may be surprised to discover that springs rather than explosions are used to provide the necessary force. The bang is a firework let off to make it look like the cannon had really fired.

5 And did you know we've got springs in our legs too? The ligaments that hold your joints together are a bit springy and your "S" shaped backbone jogs up and down as you walk. Together they'll put a spring in your step.

6 In the 1970s two American scientists trained a pair of kangaroos to hop on a treadmill. The scientists found that kangaroos jump using their springy tendons. It's a bit like jumping on a pogo stick.

7 Springy things are important for sport. Traditional tennis rackets were very expensive and strung with springy sheep's guts. Sounds like a bit of a racket. And talking about springy sports equipment, trainers have to be springy too.

Super springy shoes

HAS ANYONE SEEN MY TRAINERS?

SMELLY PONG

MIDSOLE - NICE SPRINGY BUBBLES

RUBBER LAYER - GOOD FOR PROVIDING FRICTION TO GRIP THE GROUND

Do this to your brother's trainers and you better run for it before he takes a swing at you. Funnily enough the next chapter's about swinging and spinning too. Better stand clear.

FASCINATING!

Getting in a Spin

Ever wondered why cars don't have square wheels? No – me neither. Well – round wheels go round better (howls of amazement). Also the force on the outer parts of the wheel produces greater force at the axle. And this is ideal for wheel-based machines such as waterwheels and cars. And there's lots more wheel-life facts to go around (and pathetic jokes too)…

Fatal forces expressions

STOP IT! IT'S CONSERVATION OF ANGULAR MOMENTUM!

Who's to blame?

Answer:

No one – his 10p is rolling away. He's describing how coins and any other spinning objects have a habit of turning until another force gets in the way. That's why wheels work so well. Best put your foot over the coin and pretend you haven't seen it. And wheels **are** wonderful. They were invented by some bright spark who lived in the Middle East in about 3500 BC. When a wheel goes round you get two different forces at work. Centripetal (sen-tree-pea-tal) and centrifugal (sen-tree-few-gal) forces. Confused? Let's face the facts – it's complicated. But it's worth giving it a whirl.

NAME: Centrifugal and centripetal forces

THE BASIC FACTS:
Imagine whirling a
small ball round your
head on a bit of string.

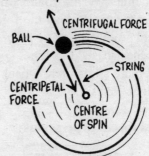

1. Centrifugal force
tries to throw the ball
off in a straight line.

2. Centripetal force is the opposite. It tries to
pull the ball inwards towards the centre of its spin.

O.K. – SO I NEED
TO PRACTICE A
BIT MORE...

THE HORRIBLE DETAILS: A bolas
uses both forces for catching
animals or people. It's two balls
on a rope. You whirl the bolas
above your head and let go. The
rope winds around your target's
legs. Read on to
discover how it works.

HANG ON, WHICH
FORCE WAS PULLING
OUTWARDS AND WHICH
WAS PULLING IN?

If you have trouble working out which is which, this rhyme might help you.

> Centripetal's in a spin
> All the time it's pulling in
> Centrifugal's worth a try
> Let go string and watch ball's fly!

Dare you discover ... how a bolas works?

What you need:
Two balls of blu-tak each 2.5 cm across
A piece of strong string or twine 52 cm long

What you do:
1 Wrap a ball of blu-tak around each end of the string.
2 Squeeze the blu-tak to make sure it is holding the string securely.
3 Now you can practise throwing it. Hold the string between your thumb and fingers half-way between the two balls. Whirl the string round your head. Let go.

WHIZzzz

NOTE: READ HEALTH WARNING FIRST ON PAGE 110

HORRIBLE HEALTH WARNING

1 Practising throwing your bolas indoors could be fatal for you if it knocks any priceless ornaments off the mantelpiece. Much better to practise outside in a wide open space.

2 Try to resist the temptation to throw your bolas at a small brother/sister/cat/dog, even if it is in the interest of science. You could use a small tree for target practice instead.

From your observations how does the bolas work?
a) Centripetal force makes the bolas fly off in a straight line. Centrifugal force helps the bolas wrap round the tree.
b) Centrifugal force makes the bolas fly off in a straight line. Centripetal force wraps the bolas round the tree.
c) Centrifugal force makes the bolas fly away at first, but centripetal force makes it come back like a boomerang.

Answer:
b) When you release the string, centrifugal force makes the bolas fly off at high speed in a straight line. When the string hits the tree the centripetal force on the string pulls the balls inwards so they wrap round the trunk.

110

Going round in circles

Between them centripetal and centrifugal forces keep the show on the road and ensure that wheels are an all-round success story. They're useful for cars and trains, and buses and bikes, and tractors and windmills, and capstans that raise anchors. And thousands of other things too. Here are some amazing uses for wheels.

Weird wheels

1 The big Ferris wheels you see in funfairs were first invented in Russia in the 1600s. They were said to be inspired by the custom of giving children rides in the wheels used to scoop water from rivers. Too much centrifugal force and the children would be thrown into the river.

2 The name actually comes from American showman George Ferris who built a 75 metre-wheel in 1893. Trouble is it took all of 20 minutes to go round once. Not much centrifugal force there.

3 Wacky inventor Joseph Merlin gate-crashed a London party to show off the roller skates he'd just invented. The eighteenth-century boffin glided along playing his violin and feeling dead cool as he swished across the polished floor. Until he found he couldn't stop and crashed into a mirror. Merlin's problem was that his wheels spun easily on the smooth floor. And there wasn't much friction to slow them down. Bet he was really cut up about it.

4 By turning a wheel you can produce a force that can be used to power all kinds of machines. In the nineteenth century prisoners were put on the treadmill. They had to climb a revolting revolving wheel but they never reached the top because the wheel kept turning towards them. In the rotting prison ships the treadmills operated the pumps that stopped the ship sinking!

Bet you never knew!

Centrifugal force ISN'T a real force – it just feels like one. It's really another example of Newton's Third Law – the one about things wanting to go off in a straight line. So when you see a cowboy film and the cowboy waves a lasso and lets it fly through the air, remember. The lasso is being powered by force that doesn't officially exist!

WELL IT FEELS REAL ENOUGH TO ME

Test your teacher

This is such a simple test that even a teacher ought to get 50 per cent right – just by guessing – 'cos there are only two possible answers. Centrifugal force and centripetal force. Easy – innit?

1 The force used in labs to separate red blood cells from the rest of the blood.

2 The reason a pendulum swings more slowly in Central Africa than in Europe. (This is true.)

3 The force that keeps your bike on the road when you lean over to go round a corner.

4 The reason that you can whiz upside-down on a roller-coaster and not fall out even if you weren't strapped in.

5 The force that stops a spacecraft falling down.

6 The force inside a rotor. That's the theme park ride that whirls you around as the floor drops away leaving you stuck to the wall.

Answers:

1 Centrifugal force. The machine is called a centrifuge. It consists of a wheel on which a container is secured. The wheel whirls round hundreds of times a minute and the heavier cells in the blood sink to the bottom. A centrifuge is also used to separate the lighter cream from the rest of the milk. And they don't use the same machine!

2 Centrifugal force. There's a special bonus point if your teacher can explain how it works. As the Earth spins round, centrifugal force makes its middle, the equator, bulge slightly. And this makes gravity slightly stronger here than elsewhere. The slight difference explains the pendulum puzzle. Newton suggested this amazing answer and he was proved right in 1735 when the French government sent expeditions to Peru and Lapland to swing pendulums and compare the results.

3 Centripetal force. Centrifugal force is the force that throws you off unless you lean over slightly as you turn.

4 Centrifugal force keeps you in place as long as you keep moving. Stop and you'll fall out – which is why it's essential to be strapped in.

5 Centrifugal force. It's the same effect as the roller-coaster. The spacecraft is falling all the time under the influence of gravity but its momentum pushes it in a straight line. The result of these two forces is that the spacecraft carries on flying round the Earth.

6 It's centripetal force caused by the wall pushing against you as you whiz round.

Teacher's tea-break teaser

If you are feeling madly brave, knock on the staffroom door. When it groans, creaks, or scrapes open, smile sweetly at your teacher and say:

EXCUSE ME, I WAS WONDERING WHY WHEN YOU STIR YOUR TEA, THE TEA LEAVES SETTLE AT THE CENTRE OF THE BOTTOM OF YOUR TEA CUP? SURELY CENTRIFUGAL FORCE SHOULD PUSH THE LEAVES TOWARDS THE SIDES?

Answer: Incredibly two of the world's greatest scientists puzzled over this for years. That's Nobel prize winners Albert Einstein (1879–1955) and Erwin Schrödinger (1887–1961). In 1926 Mrs S asked Erwin the question but he didn't know the answer. So she asked Einstein. After many calculations Einstein worked out the answer and even wrote an article about it in 1933.

According to Einstein centrifugal force does push the tea leaves towards the sides of the cup. But friction between the liquid and the sides slows down the tea leaves at the sides and base of the cup. This weakens the centrifugal force. And as the liquid stops turning the leaves fall towards the centre of the cup. Wow! And you thought it was just a cup of tea! Here's another amazing story to keep things swinging.

Getting in the swing

It was 1586 and 17-year-old Galileo (yes, him again) was in Pisa Cathedral listening to a boring sermon. He noticed a chandelier swinging in the breeze. Sometimes it swung in a long arc and sometimes in a shorter swing. But each swing seemed to take the same time.

So Galileo timed the swings using his pulse. He was right. (Could you make a similar discovery during a boring science lesson?)

Galileo used this newly discovered fact to design a new kind of clock. The grandfather clock used a swinging pendulum to keep time. What a time-ly invention.

In 1650 two priests spent a whole day counting the swings of a pendulum in a bid to prove the pendulum really did keep time. It did and they counted 87,998 swings.

But one sickly scientist had even bigger pendulum plans.

Hall of Fame: Jean Bernard Léon Foucault
(1819–1868) Nationality: French

Young Jean was a sickly child. And his parents reckoned school would finish him off, so they educated him at home. Why can't all parents be so considerate? Poor Jean was never any good at his lessons. For a time he went nowhere. His bid to become a surgeon failed after he ran away from an operation. One squirt of blood and a bit of suffering and wimpy Jean burst into tears.

But Jean loved writing. So he became a science journalist instead. Then he got interested in experiments. He measured the speed of light and tried to photograph the stars. He then became fascinated by the idea that you could use a pendulum to prove the Earth turned during the day. Although everyone knew this, no one had ever tried to prove it actually happened.

118

In 1851 Jean devised an amazing test. He hung a huge steel ball 60 cm in diameter and weighing 30.4 kg from the dome of the Pántheon in Paris, a large building where many famous people were buried.

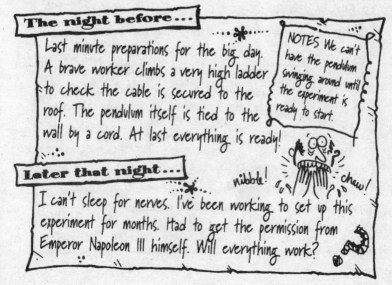

The night before...

Last minute preparations for the big day. A brave worker climbs a very high ladder to check the cable is secured to the roof. The pendulum itself is tied to the wall by a cord. At last everything is ready!

NOTES We can't have the pendulum swinging around until the experiment is ready to start.

Later that night...

nibble!   chew!

I can't sleep for nerves. I've been working to set up this experiment for months. Had to get the permission from Emperor Napoleon III himself. Will everything work?

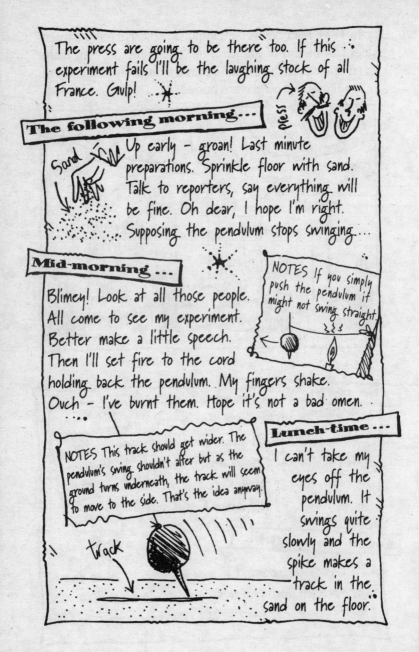

The press are going to be there too. If this ∴ experiment fails I'll be the laughing stock of all France. Gulp! ✱

The following morning...

Sand Up early – groan! Last minute preparations. Sprinkle floor with sand. Talk to reporters, say everything will be fine. Oh dear, I hope I'm right. Supposing the pendulum stops swinging...

Mid-morning ...

Blimey! Look at all those people. All come to see my experiment. Better make a little speech. Then I'll set fire to the cord holding back the pendulum. My fingers shake. Ouch – I've burnt them. Hope it's not a bad omen.

NOTES If you simply push the pendulum it might not swing straight.

NOTES This track should get wider. The pendulum's swing shouldn't alter but as the ground turns underneath, the track will seem to move to the side. That's the idea anyway.

track

Lunch-time ...

I can't take my eyes off the pendulum. It swings quite slowly and the spike makes a track in the sand on the floor.

Still swinging. Time seems to drag. I count the swings. It's like counting sheep.
I'm dozing off. Yawn - should have got more sleep last night. Zzzzzzzzzzzz

Still swinging. Nothing happening. I should have known this right from the start. Maybe I could push the pendulum to one side when no one's looking. Help! The Emperor's glaring at me and he's really cross. I'M FINISHED. PANIC STATIONS!!!!

Nap III glaring

← Still sleeping

Just then ...
I open my eyes. Phew! It must have been a dream. Everyone's pointing to the sand and talking. THE TRACK HAS GOT WIDER. I'M SAVED!!!

The world really does go round. YIPPEEEEE! I feel like dancing about and kissing everyone.

121

Foucault found himself a hero. He was awarded the *Légion d'Honneur* medal. He went on to invent gyroscopes ... which work on the same principle as tops as you'll see in a moment. And tops are top toys for freaky physicists.

Top tricks

Physicists like nothing better than playing with their favourite toys. Well, according to them they're investigating forces. Oh, yeah.

There are loads of toys that use the forces of spinning. Toys like, yo-yos, hula-hoops, frisbees. And tops. A top was a favourite toy of Nobel prize winner Wolfgang Pauli (1900–1958) who was trying to work out the physics of inertia. Here's some crucial info to get *you* "tops" of the class.

Tops balance because angular momentum keeps them going – remember the coin running away from the scientist? Tops keep turning in the same way despite the efforts of gravity to pull them down. Bigger tops need more effort to get going but spin for longer. Tops are popular with kids the world over. Here's a traditional Inuit game you might like to play when it gets really cold.

What you need:

IGLOO

SPINNING TOP

Spin the top. Run round your igloo (or house). Try to get back inside before the top falls down. (This could be fatal if you don't wrap up warm first.)

YOU ONLY HAVE TO GO ROUND ONCE!

In 1743 English inventor John Smeaton (1724–1794) invented a sort of top that would stay level even on a ship in a storm. This allowed mariners to check where the horizon should be. They could then work out the positions of the sun and stars to navigate by. But the new fangled top didn't catch on because seafarers were useless at spinning it.

But Smeaton's brainwave was the ancestor of gyroscopes found on most ships and planes today.

Foucault's invention – the gyroscope – works like a series of tops. They balance on one another and always stay upright. And this is ideal if you want to steer a steady course. Amazingly, your bike wheels work in much the same way. When they spin round the bike is much less likely tip over than when it's stationary. Scientists call this "precession". Something to think about next time you go for a precession on your bike.

Bet you never knew!
The tighter your circle of spin the faster you go. That's why ice-skaters pull in their arms to spin faster. It's the law of conservation of angular momentum again. Because the circle of spin is smaller they go round quicker. This fact also explains why water speeds up near the centre of a whirlpool. You can check this fact by watching the dregs of your washing-up gurgle down the plug hole. And if this isn't your idea of fun you'd better dive into the next chapter. You'll soon get your bounce back.

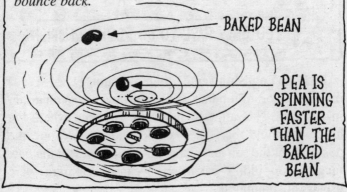

BAKED BEAN

PEA IS SPINNING FASTER THAN THE BAKED BEAN

Bouncing back

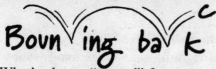

What's always "around" for a game and doesn't mind a good kicking? No, not your sports teacher. It's a *ball*. And oddly enough balls do other forceful things. Like rolling and spinning and bouncing. Here are a few facts to bounce off your friends.

Fatal forces fact file

NAME: Bouncing

THE BASIC FACTS: When a rubber ball hits the floor the springy coiled rubber molecules that make up the ball are all squashed together. They soak up the energy of the impact and then bounce out again – making the ball bounce.

THE HORRIBLE DETAILS: The first chewing gum was made of chicle, a type of tree sap. American scientists tried to make the chicle into a type of rubber but it wasn't bouncy enough. So they just chewed the problem over, or rather chewed the chicle.

Keep your eye on the ball

When a ball flies through the air, strange things start to happen. Scientists have put loads of effort into working out what these mysterious effects are.

Fatal forces fact file

NAME: Flying balls

THE BASIC FACTS: When you throw or kick a ball friction with the air causes drag and this slows the ball. At the same time it's hit by turbulence. That's when spinning masses of air form around the ball and give it bumpy ride.

THE HORRIBLE DETAILS: A baseball can be pitched at 145km per hour (90 mph). That's fatally fast for anyone in the way without protective gear.

Any old scientist will tell you that ball games involve forces. So we invited our pet scientist along to show you how science can help you improve at sports such as tennis. According to the scientist you don't need to work up a sweat. All you need is a few brain cells and a small computer. *Oh, yeah?*

The scientist's guide to tennis

Tennis ball seams are the same on each side. This means equal amounts of air turbulence. So the ball flies straight. That's quite a velocity. Slice the racket downwards and you'll get back-spin. The ball tumbles backwards as it flies forwards. This drags air over it. As this air speeds up, the pressure above the ball drops and the greater air pressure under the ball raises it. We call this effect, lift.

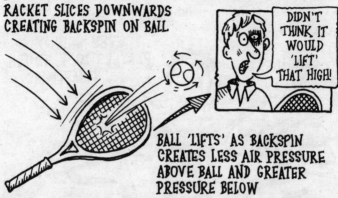

RACKET SLICES DOWNWARDS CREATING BACKSPIN ON BALL

DIDN'T THINK IT WOULD 'LIFT' THAT HIGH!

BALL 'LIFTS' AS BACKSPIN CREATES LESS AIR PRESSURE ABOVE BALL AND GREATER PRESSURE BELOW

Top spin is the opposite. Strike the ball upwards and the ball tumbles forwards as it flies forwards. This drags air under the ball. And as it speeds up the pressure drops and the ball is pushed lower and it bounces faster.

DIDN'T THINK IT WOULD BOUNCE THAT FAST!

RACKET MOVES UPWARDS CREATING TOP SPIN.

BALL BOUNCES FASTER AS TOPSPIN CREATES MORE AIR PRESSURE ABOVE THE BALL AND LESS BELOW

If you hit the ball a glancing blow it bounces extra slowly when it hits the ground. So it's even easier to whack.

Painless padding
If you find games a pain in the sports bag maybe you need a bit more protection. Here's a few bits and pieces of equipment designed to help you play safe.

• Cushioned shoulder padding and shin pads as worn by American footballers.

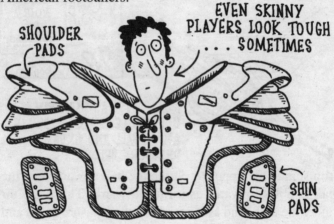

SHOULDER PADS

EVEN SKINNY PLAYERS LOOK TOUGH ... SOMETIMES

SHIN PADS

• Boxer's gum shield. Stops teeth from being knocked out of their sockets.

NO PROBLEM

• American footballer's helmet. Cage to protect face.

CAGE TO PROTECT FACE

UNBREAKABLE PLASTIC

• Dome shape spreads force of blow over whole helmet. Stops head from getting squashed.
• Cricketer's box to protect the vulnerable bits. Very useful – cricket balls travel at 160 km per hour (100 mph).

HOWZAT!

PAINFUL!

WITH BOX

WITHOUT BOX

Here are a few more facts to prove that science really is a ball.

Having a ball
1 The first balls were made by the Romans from bits of dead animal skin stitched together and filled with air.

Later on in the Middle Ages balls were made from pig's bladders filled with air. Yuck – who had to blow them up?

IMPORTANT!
REMEMBER TO EMPTY THE BLADDER FIRST

2 The first golf balls were leather bags packed with boiled chicken's feathers. Bet that made the feathers fly. The balls flew very well until it rained when they soon got waterlogged and split. Covering the players in grotty old feathers.

3 In the 1850s someone had the idea of making golf balls out of rubbery tree sap. But they didn't fly as straight as the old balls until they became scratched and worn. Then they flew really well.

4 So what was going on? Turned out the rough surface of the golf ball trapped tiny pockets of air. The turbulent air flowed around the trapped air and this actually gave a smoother quicker flight. And that's why modern golf balls have little dimples.

5 Cricket balls also do strange things as they fly through the air. Normally the ball just spins horizontally. But at speed, air turbulence makes the ball swerve if the edge of the ball's seam is smooth. That's why some cricketers polish the ball by rubbing it on their trousers.

6 At speeds of 100 km (62 mph) plus, the ball can swerve even more. Especially if the edge of the seam is rough. And that's why some cricketers rub dirt into the ball. But don't do this in your games lesson – it's called cheating.

7 The ball used in rugby and American football has pointed ends. If it's tumbling forward it can bounce oddly. Sometimes it bounces high, sometimes low.

8 This makes it tricky to pick up. And dangerous too unless you enjoy 20 giant people jumping on your head. The good news is that the ball is easier to throw. Pitch it with one end pointing forwards and it'll spin horizontally like an over-sized bullet. This means you can easily get rid of it before you get flattened. It's safer than just standing and juggling the ball…

Dare you discover … how to juggle?
Juggling is a great way to see how forces affect balls in the air. Tell your gullible folks you're doing your homework. Then you can have a bit of fun.

What you will need:

Yourself

Something to juggle with. Three balls small enough to fit in your hands would be good. Or you could try rolled up socks

Plenty of space

A mirror

Safety note: When you are learning to juggle try to resist the urge to use your granny's priceless antiques, food (especially at meal-times), and living creatures such as hamsters, goldfish, small brothers and sisters, etc.

1 Stand in front of a mirror with your elbows tucked close to your body and your hands level with your waist. Place your legs apart with your knees slightly bent. Easy, isn't it? Are you ready?

ADOPT A CONFIDENT AND RELAXED EXPRESSION

REMAIN CALM AND STILL

2 Take a deep breath and let it out slowly. That's right – relax. Now without looking at your hands … throw the ball gently up and over your head. Notice how it falls in an arc under the influence of gravity just like the cannonballs Galileo studied – remember? Catch the ball in the palm of your other hand. Keep your eyes in the top part of the ball's flight. OK – that's the easy bit.

3 Now it gets a bit harder. Juggling with two balls takes a bit of practice. Throw one ball up as before. When the ball is just about to drop, throw your second ball up from the other hand. Ideally the second ball should pass just under the first ball.

4 OK, this takes practice. Better practise now to get it right.

5 This is where it gets *really* hard. Three balls. Sure you want to try? OK. Hold two balls in one hand and one in the other. Repeat Step 3.

6 Now here's the clever bit. When ball 2 is just about to drop throw ball 3 up and try to get it to pass under ball 2.

Meanwhile catch ball 1 and throw it up just when ball 3 is about to drop. Easy!

7 Fantastic, keep going!

And while you're doing this, here are some interesting facts to juggle with.

1 The most balls anyone has ever managed to juggle was 10. This feat was achieved by several people including American Bruce Sarafian in 1996.

2 Kara, a nineteenth-century American performer used to juggle with his hat, lighted cigar, gloves, newspaper, matches and a coffee cup. Don't try this at home … or at school.

3 It's also possible to juggle with your feet. This trick was pioneered by another American performer named Derious. As long as their back is supported the performer can juggle quite weighty objects including a small child.

Sooner or later they'll invent a juggling machine. Then people could enjoy the fun of juggling without ever having to learn for themselves. That's typical of us humans. Always inventing machines to get out of hard work. There are loads more mighty machines that use forces to do work. Listen hard and you'll hear them grinding up their gears for the next chapter...

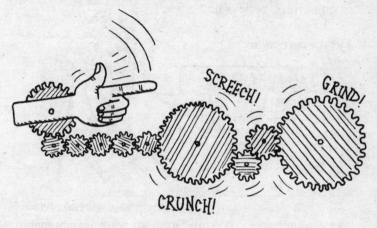

SCREECH!

GRIND!

CRUNCH!

MIGHTY MACHINES

A machine is a way of using a force in the right place to get a job done with less effort. Good idea. So why, after ten thousand years of science and invention is there no machine for doing homework? Anyway, to make a mighty machine all you need is a collection of effort-saving levers, pulleys and gears.

Fatal expressions

ARGH! ROTATIONAL INERTIA – I NEED MORE TORQUE!

Answer:
No – a mechanic. The scientist can't loosen a nut. Torque is the word scientists use to describe the turning force you produce using a spanner. Rotational inertia is the resistance of the nut to being turned. And spanners are good for doing this job because they work like levers, as you'll see.

Lovely levers

A lever is a pole that you use to lever something up or push or pull something around. Either way the lever rests on a point known as the fulcrum. Levers work because the most effective turning force is at right angles to the thing you want to move. So levers help you do more work for less effort. Lovely!

Dare you discover ... how a lever works?

What you need:
Yourself
A door

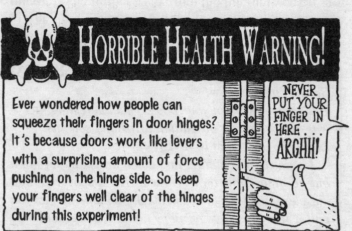

HORRIBLE HEALTH WARNING!

Ever wondered how people can squeeze their fingers in door hinges? It's because doors work like levers with a surprising amount of force pushing on the hinge side. So keep your fingers well clear of the hinges during this experiment!

NEVER PUT YOUR FINGER IN HERE ... ARGHH!

What you do:
1 Open the door slightly. Make sure no one charges through the door.
2 Stand outside the door and try to push it by pressing with one finger 2 cm from the hinges.
3 Now press with the same finger 2 cm from opposite side to the hinges.

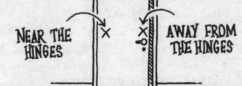

NEAR THE HINGES

AWAY FROM THE HINGES

Which is easier?
a) They're both impossible and you got a sore finger.
b) It's easier to push the door near the hinges.
c) It's easier to push the door further away from the hinges.

Answer:
c) The door works like a lever with the hinges as the fulcrum. The further away from the fulcrum you press the more forceful your push is. Nowadays you'll find levers everywhere. From typewriters to tin openers and from scissors to see-saws.

Bet you never knew!
You've got levers in your body. This interesting fact was discovered by the Italian artist and scientist Leonardo da Vinci (1452–1519).

Leonardo was cutting up human arms and legs in a bid to find how they worked. He discovered that muscles pulled the bones in much the same way as you pull a lever to move an object. He was so excited by this discovery that he even made a working model leg using copper wires and bits of real human bones. Then he could see it in action.

Teacher tea-break teaser

This playground puzzle spells break-time bafflement for your teacher. Two children are playing on a see-saw. If the little child jumps off she might get hurt. If the big child gets off he'll get a nasty injury as the see-saw swings up under the weight of the smaller child. What's to be done?

WHAT'S TO BE DONE?

FULCRUM

Powerful pulleys

Another method of lifting heavy weights off the ground – including large children – is the pulley. Basically it's a wheel hung off the ground with a rope passing over it. This re-directs force. So you can pull on the rope and lift something tied to the other end of the rope.

Add another wheel to the first one and it's even easier. By pulling the rope a longer distance you spread the effort so it seems easier to lift the load. Nowadays you'll find pulleys on cranes and lifts. So whom do we have to thank for this amazing invention? It was a Greek genius – Archimedes (287?–212 BC).

A lovely little mover

Archimedes had a little problem. His relative, Hieron, had asked him to pull a full-sized ship down a beach and out to sea – without help! Now most of us would tell the brother-in-law to jump in a vat of custard and go back to watching the telly. But Archimedes couldn't say that.

Unfortunately, Hieron was the local king – Hieron II of Syracuse to be exact. And you don't refuse royalty even if they are family. Besides, Archimedes was an all-round genius. He was supposed to know these things. He'd already worked out the maths of levers and boasted that with a long enough lever he could lift the world. Hieron thought his brainy relative should be taught a lesson. So he deliberately set him an impossible task.

Archimedes scratched his balding head and chewed his lip. All that night he worked on mathematical plans. And eventually he hit on a solution. An answer so stunningly original, so forceful and amazing that no one had ever thought of it before. A new machine. Meanwhile, hundreds of grim-faced guards grunted and groaned as they hauled the ship up the beach. Hieron ordered them to load the ship with cargo and told some of them to wait on board.

Archimedes and a few assistants spent the next few hours setting up the machine. History doesn't record what it looked like. But it must have been a series of pulleys standing on wooden frames with the rope tied securely to the ship. When all was ready Archimedes gripped the free end of the rope. He looked rather thin and weedy. Hieron couldn't resist a quiet chuckle as Archimedes rolled up his sleeves and tugged on the rope.

But then the ship slid smoothly down the beach. It moved with eerie ease as if it was sailing on a calm sea. Archimedes' machine was a lovely little mover. The watching crowds gasped in disbelief. The people on the ship looked stunned and Hieron nearly had a heart attack. If he hadn't seen it with his own eyes the king would have accused his brainy relative of pulley-ing his leg.

Grinding gears

No one knows who invented gears but the Romans certainly used them. They're interlocking toothed wheels that pass on force and they have odd sounding names that wouldn't be out of place in an ancient torture chamber. Names such as "bevels", "rack and pinion", "spurs" and "worms". They all work the same way. A smaller wheel that turns quickly and a larger wheel that turns more slowly.

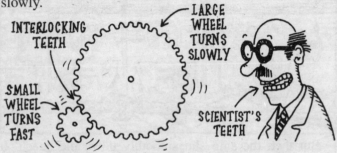

INTERLOCKING TEETH

LARGE WHEEL TURNS SLOWLY

SMALL WHEEL TURNS FAST

SCIENTIST'S TEETH

Gears increase the amount of work you get for the amount of force you put in. Take your bicycle gears, for example. The gear wheels on your bike have fewer teeth than the chain wheel. So the gear wheels turn faster and they make your rear bike wheel turn faster than you pedal. So it does you a really good turn.

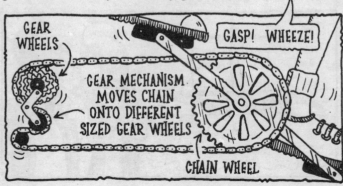

GEAR WHEELS

GASP! WHEEZE!

GEAR MECHANISM MOVES CHAIN ONTO DIFFERENT SIZED GEAR WHEELS

CHAIN WHEEL

The bicycle was such a good idea that nineteenth-century inventors began to peddle their own pedal-powered machines. Which of these are too silly to be true?

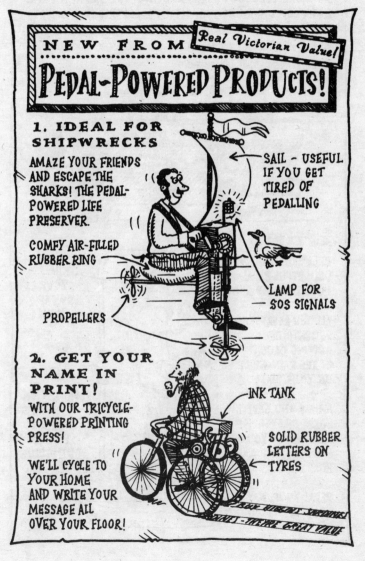

NEW FROM *Real Victorian Value!*

PEDAL-POWERED PRODUCTS!

1. IDEAL FOR SHIPWRECKS

AMAZE YOUR FRIENDS AND ESCAPE THE SHARKS! THE PEDAL-POWERED LIFE PRESERVER.

COMFY AIR-FILLED RUBBER RING

PROPELLERS

SAIL - USEFUL IF YOU GET TIRED OF PEDALLING

LAMP FOR SOS SIGNALS

2. GET YOUR NAME IN PRINT!

WITH OUR TRICYCLE-POWERED PRINTING PRESS!

WE'LL CYCLE TO YOUR HOME AND WRITE YOUR MESSAGE ALL OVER YOUR FLOOR!

INK TANK

SOLID RUBBER LETTERS ON TYRES

3. DON'T MISS OUR BUS!

NO MORE SCHOOL BUS BREAKDOWNS. TRY THE NEW PEDAL-POWERED SCHOOL BUS. SPECIAL PEDALS UNDER THE SEATS LINKED TO A ROTATING CRANKSHAFT POWER THE BUS AT 35KM PER HOUR (22 MPH).

"GETS THE KIDS TO SCHOOL ON TIME AND KEEPS THEM FIT."
I. FLOGGEM (HEADMASTER)

4. TIRED OUT?

RELAX UNDER OUR DELIGHTFUL PEDAL-POWERED COLD SHOWER!

ALL THE REFRESHING DELIGHTS OF GETTING CAUGHT IN THE RAIN WHILE ON YOUR BIKE!

A NEW AND EXCITING FORM OF EXERCISE THAT LEAVES YOU FEELING FRESH AND FIT.

PEDAL YOUR WAY TO A CLEAN BODY!

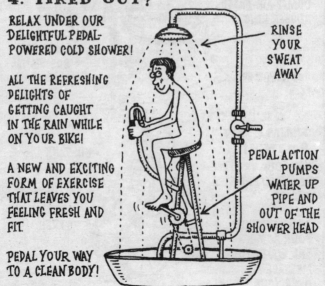

RINSE YOUR SWEAT AWAY

PEDAL ACTION PUMPS WATER UP PIPE AND OUT OF THE SHOWER HEAD

Marvellous mighty machines

A complicated machine is simply lots of simple machines joined together. Easy. Just a load of old screws, pulleys, levers, gears, wheels, axles, chains, transmission shafts and springs that you just happen to find lying about in the garage. Throw them all together and everything should go like clockwork.

From bikes and gears it's a small step to steam engines, petrol engines, trains, buses, cars and planes. Just think. If it wasn't for forces they wouldn't be able to force you to go to school. Terrible. Still, you can relax at home, can't you? No need to worry about forces is there? Safe as houses and all that … er – well, actually, forces *can* be fatal for buildings, too. The next chapter will really shake you up.

ACTUALLY, THE GARDEN COULD DO WITH A DROP OF RAIN

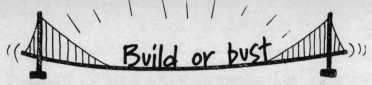

Fallen down under the influence of gravity, blown down, blown up or just shaken about. Yep. Forces are fatal for buildings, too.

Bodge-it buildings

Some buildings stand for hundreds of years. Others stand for hundreds of days ... or minutes.

Would you be interested in buying any of these structures?

Go Undercover!

THE KEMPER ARENA, Kansas City, USA (built 1973)

▶ Spectacular covered all-weather sports stadium. Keeps that nasty rain off your head.

▶ Winner of an architectural award in 1976.

▶ Cost $23.3 million (£14 million) to build.

THE SMALL PRINT
In 1979 the roof of the Kemper Arena fell in after heavy rain. Engineers believe rainwater collected on the roof making it sag until its supports couldn't take the weight any longer.

ARGHHH!

HELP!

I CAN'T SWIM!

WAT-ER GREAT BRIDGE!

LONDON BRIDGE, Spanning the River Thames in London on 20 narrow arches. (built 1176-1209)

DON'T DIG THE GRAVE THERE!

ARGHH!

▶ Waterwheels and shops.

▶ Sensational tidal surges through the narrow arches.

▶ All this and the dead body of the architect, Peter Colechurch. He's buried in the chapel on the bridge.

▶ Complete with drawbridge and spikes for traitors' rotting heads.

ROTTEN TRAITOR

THE SMALL PRINT

The arches were narrow and close together, and this forced the river to surge violently. This damaged the bridge and made life dangerous for boatmen. Up to fifty were killed each year trying to pass under the bridge. Part of the bridge fell down in 1281 and again in 1482. It was finally knocked down in 1832. Peter Colechurch should have designed his bridge with wider arches to allow the water to flow more easily. He should also have banned buildings on the bridge itself because their weight was too great for the bridge to bear.

GO WITH A SWING!

THE TACOMA NARROWS BRIDGE, Washington State, USA (built 1940)

▶ A graceful lightweight suspension bridge. (That's a bridge supported by cables hung from towers.)

▶ Amazing 853 metre (2,800 foot) span.

▶ Swings about in the wind for a really exciting crossing.

THE SMALL PRINT

The Tacoma Narrows Bridge swayed so violently in the wind that it earned the nickname "Galloping Gertie". People actually felt seasick crossing it. The bridge had to be reinforced to stop the swaying spreading to the towers that held up the cables. But four months later a strong wind twisted the roadway sideways until it collapsed.

When a building falls down many people can be killed. But the biggest death-tolls happen when dams burst. A dam has to hold back the huge force of water that builds up against it. That's why dams have such thick walls and are often built in a strong arch shape so the water presses the dam into the sides of the valley rather than backwards. But sometimes this isn't enough. In 1975 flooding burst two dams in Henan province in China and 235,000 people were washed away. So you can see how important it is for all architects to be properly trained. If you'd like to be a good architect you'd better pay attention to these simple rules...

Become an architect in six easy lessons
Lesson 1: Understand the effect of forces on your building

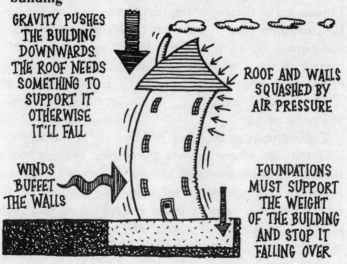

GRAVITY PUSHES THE BUILDING DOWNWARDS. THE ROOF NEEDS SOMETHING TO SUPPORT IT OTHERWISE IT'LL FALL

ROOF AND WALLS SQUASHED BY AIR PRESSURE

WINDS BUFFET THE WALLS

FOUNDATIONS MUST SUPPORT THE WEIGHT OF THE BUILDING AND STOP IT FALLING OVER

Nowadays architects make computer simulations and models of their buildings and even test the models in wind tunnels.

Lesson 2: Develop an eye for forces

A good architect or engineer can look at a building and spot whether the building is well built enough to stand up to the forces on it. Marc Brunel (that's Isambard's dad) once looked at a bridge in Paris and said:

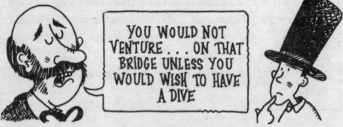

YOU WOULD NOT VENTURE . . . ON THAT BRIDGE UNLESS YOU WOULD WISH TO HAVE A DIVE

Three days later, the bridge collapsed. Yep, old Marc kept dry and he certainly had a dry sense of humour too.

Lesson 3: Put in proper foundations

If you've ever tried to carry some tall glasses on a tray one-handed like a waiter, you'll know how tricky it is to balance them. It would help if the glasses were partly buried in a really thick tray. That's how foundations work. The taller the building the deeper the foundations you need.

Foundations stop the wind from blowing your building over and they support the weight of your building too. Remember Galileo working at Pisa University? In 1173 Pisa's bell tower was built on soft ground with foundations that weren't broad enough to support its weight. Now Pisa University's famous for its learning and the tower's famous for its leaning.

Lesson 4: Always build your building the right shape
Triangles are a good strong shape. That's why the Egyptian pyramids have lasted 4,700 years. The Eiffel Tower was also made up of a series of triangles and many modern skyscrapers use triangles as the basis of their metal frames.

A column is a good strong shape and ideal for holding up heavy weights. Like the roof, for example. You can use arches to hold up part of the walls. Like columns, arches are great because the harder you push down on them the more they push back. Yes – it's Newton's Third Law again.

Dome shapes are also very strong. But you knew that from finding out about helmets in Chapter 3. An egg shape is also surprisingly strong and can take a weight of 22.7 kg. But don't try leaving an egg on your teacher's chair.

Lesson 5: Make sure your walls don't fall down

If you are designing a very tall stone building you may choose to make your walls very thick like an old cathedral or castle – the walls of the Tower of London are more than 4.6 metres thick. So you want to put in larger windows but you know they will weaken your walls. No problem. Try using buttresses to hold your walls up.

Mind you, disasters do happen. In 1989 the Civic Tower in Pavia, Italy (built 1060) fell with a crash. The cement holding the stones together had slowly crumbled away. Engineers reckoned that the shock waves from years of ringing the bells at the top had brought on the destruction. If this puts you off building in stone you could use a strong steel frame for your tall building and use lighter materials for your walls. This makes them stronger but the building might sway a bit in windy weather.

Lesson 6: Get your roof the right shape

Roofs are usually sloping because the curved shape is more difficult to bend. You can prove this by holding a piece of paper in different ways.

HOLD IT LIKE THIS AND IT'S FLOPPY

BUT HOLD THE PAPER LIKE THIS AND ITS STRAIGHT.

Vicious vibes

One thing that can be very destructive is vibration. Have you ever watched a washing machine shuddering and shaking as it washes and spins the clothes. Perhaps you've bravely laid a finger on the machine and felt the shaking passing up your arms. These are vibrations. And beware. They can be vicious.

TRAPPING YOUR TIE COULD PROVE FATAL...

Fatal expressions

Should you dial 999? No, her car's shuddering with vibrations. Probably because it's so clapped out. Oscillatory motion is in fact what vibrations are called. Oscillations are regularly repeated movements or shaking. The only way to stop them is to "damp them down". No, this doesn't mean chucking water over the car. Still confused? Well, it means using some soft substance to absorb the vibrations and stop the shuddering.

Vicious vibration facts

Vibrations are particularly vicious in their effects on buildings and bridges. In 1850, 487 soldiers were marching across a suspension bridge in Algiers in Africa. Their heavy boots thudded on the roadway. And soon the whole bridge was shaking with the vibrations. It shook so much that bits fell off it and finally the entire bridge collapsed into the river. Tragically 226 soldiers were killed.

Ever since, soldiers avoid marching in step when they cross a bridge in order not set off the deadly vibrations.

That takes a bit of foresight but sometimes it pays to plan the crossing of your bridges before you come to them. Mind you, the most vicious vibrations aren't caused by people – they're caused by the Earth itself.

Every year there are hundreds of earthquakes. Some of them are fatal for people. Movement of vast rocky areas deep under the ground trigger powerful vibrations in the form of shock waves that can destroy entire cities. The damage is done because shock waves make the walls vibrate so violently that the building falls down. Feeling a little shaky?

Dare you discover ... how much your body vibrates?
What you need:
Yourself
A 30 cm ruler
A large eraser or small weight

What you do:
1 Place the eraser on the end of ruler.
2 Grip the opposite end of the ruler by your thumb and forefinger. Then hold the ruler as close to its end as you can.
3 Stretch out your hand balancing the eraser on the opposite end of the ruler.

What do you notice?
a) Nothing. I did the test for ten minutes and my hand was steady as a rock.
b) After a few seconds the end of the ruler began to dance around as my arm twitched.
c) I lost my balance and fell over forwards.

A smashing finale

Now you've learnt about how forces affect buildings, let's practise using forces to knock one down. An old school will do. Imagine your school has been condemned as an unsafe building. Perhaps all those hundreds of feet stomping up and down the corridors has triggered vicious vibrations that have fatally weakened the building. Now your school must be flattened. No more science lessons – that's really tough. Oh well – here's how to do the demolition job…

1 Make sure that the school is empty of all pupils and there are no teachers lurking in the corners. You wouldn't want to knock the building down on top of them would you?

2 Start off by swinging a heavy steel ball against the walls of your school. The ball transfers its momentum to the wall as it crashes into it. Cement is dislodged from the bricks and the wall falls down.

3 If you don't have a steel ball you'll have to smash the walls with a sledge hammer. This has the same effect but it's far slower and much harder work.

4 Some buildings have pre-stressed concrete beams. These are concrete beams with steel wires running through them. The wires are held tight by the weight of the building's upper floors. Be careful if your school has these beams. When you knock down the upper floors the wires in the lower floor's beams aren't held tight any more. So they go *ping* and the entire building crashes down around your ears.

Alternatively you could try one of these demolition methods.

Method 1. Explosives

In a hurry? Want to knock your school down before science class on Monday? You could blow it up. Place explosive charges around the building and weaken the supporting beams so they collapse easily. Set off the explosives and wait for the dust to clear!

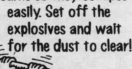

Method 2. Hands

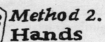

If you can't blow up your school, try using your bare hands instead. A karate blow is forceful enough to break bricks. In 1994 fifteen karate experts demolished a seven room house in Saskatchewan, Canada. Using only their bare feet and hands.

Forces were around long before we got here. And although we try to use forces – in the end we can't control them. We can only forecast what forces might do to new buildings or cars. And although designers make fatal mistakes, these embarrassing slip-ups are thankfully rare.

THE DESIGN IS FINE – YOU'VE GOT THE PLANS UPSIDE DOWN

Meanwhile, physicists are making more brain-boggling discoveries about forces. Before Galileo and Newton, no one knew how forces worked. Today we know more about them than ever. And because forces affect so much of our world, they pop up in every area of scientific knowledge.

Take atoms, for example. Scientists are probing how forces hold an atom together. (Atoms are the tiny bits of matter that make up everything in the universe.) The trick is to smash the atoms together in awesome machines called accelerators tens of kilometres long. Then you sift the debris for clues. If you're a scientist it sometimes pays to think small, ha ha.

Forces also come into space travel. To plan a little trip around the solar system you need to know how a planet's gravity will pull your craft. And how as you whiz past the planet, centrifugal force hurls you into the depths of space. All you need is an advanced computer to cope with the necessary maths.

Other physicists are looking into how gravity itself works. Are there really tiny things, even smaller than atoms, called gravitons that are somehow involved? And once scientists have found this out, could they perhaps defeat gravity and make planes that hover effortlessly in the air?

And even if we don't crack this one – there's always something new. Like a really wacky new sport. Take sky-surfing, for example. To do this you have to be seriously off your trolley. It involves jumping from an aeroplane strapped to a board. You enjoy some mid-air acrobatics before your parachute opens – assuming it does.

But one thing is certain – humans will go on pushing forces to their limits and scientists will go on studying how forces work. After all there may be limits to our knowledge, but our curiosity knows no bounds. Yep. You're forced to admit it. Forces are horribly intriguing. Fatally fascinating. But that's Horrible Science for you!

THE FIGHT FOR FLIGHT

INTRODUCTION

This foolish man is about to test a dodgy home-made pair of wings…

Well, what do you expect? Humans aren't designed to fly – as you can find out in this book. It's called *The Fight for Flight* because it tells the story of the battle to build flying machines. We'll be reliving the terror, the triumphs and the tears, and finding out why hundreds of people got killed. Our route will cover…

• The death-defying facts about flying.
• The blood-curdling blunders of barmy balloons and awesome airships.
• The fearsome flops of human-powered flight.
• The dreadful downfalls of grisly gliders (aeroplanes without engines).
• The plane-crazy perils of aeroplanes, jets and hair-raising helicopters.
• And the fateful future of flight.

This book's sure to be scary and exciting, and by the time you've finished it, you'll have logged more fearsome facts than the average teacher tots up in a lifetime. But afterwards you may find yourself thinking more about flight – and even whether air travel is a good thing…

We'll be taking off very soon, but first here are a few vital safety announcements…

THIS BOOK INCLUDES GRISLY GRUESOME BITS. YOU MAY WANT TO KEEP YOUR SICK BAG HANDY!

Another safety warning…
This book is designed for reading only and should not be used as…

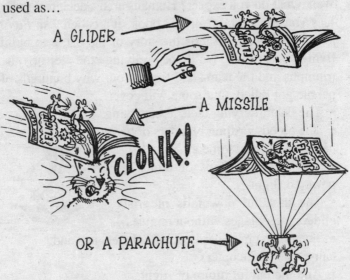

A GLIDER

A MISSILE

CLONK!

OR A PARACHUTE

There is some science in this book, but it's been cushioned with lots of jokes to stop it damaging your brain too much.

Yet another safety warning...

We'd like to warn readers that it's a very BAD idea to try to copy the crazy people and stupid stunts in this book. Yes, only airheads prance around on the wings of an aircraft 1,000 metres in the air. And as for leaping off tall buildings armed with a pair of feathery wings ... that's only suitable for bird-brains.

Provided you follow these warnings, this book is perfectly safe to read. You may feel an urge to giggle – but this is perfectly normal. In fact, the jokes have been tested on teachers and, although rather old, they're very reliable (and that goes for the jokes too!).

Well, thank you for listening... You are now cleared to fly. So, if you'll kindly fasten your safety belt and turn the page, we can take to the air...

Have a HORRIBLE flight!

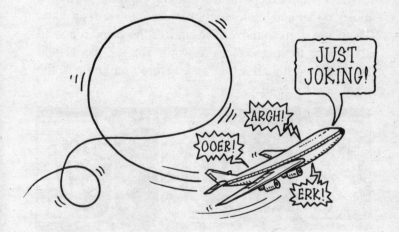

DEATH-DEFYING FLYING FACTS

This chapter is all about why planes fly and don't flop out of the sky like soggy pancakes. But before we get to grips with their soaraway secrets, let's check out how it feels to fly...

The date: TODAY
The time: EVENING
The place: ANY AIRPORT IN THE WORLD
You're about to fly. Your plane waits on the runway like a high jumper ready for their run-up.

How do you feel? Tense? Nervous? Just a teeny-weeny bit scared? Will the plane *really* fly? you worry. Or will it plummet from the sky with a crash, a bang and a splat? And how can anything as heavy as a plane fly anyway?

All is silent except for the whining engines. Then they moan louder and louder until they set your teeth on edge. The plane starts to move. The engines throb and roar, and all at once the plane races forward. You see the airfield hurtle past – it's all a blur and, before you know it, the plane soars upwards.

Your ears pop as the ground drops away and the plane climbs towards the rolling clouds. Then, all at once, you're as high as the clouds and the ground is a map seen from above. Up in the dark evening sky, a lone star gleams…

Yes – flying is magic! I mean when you fly you get to see loads of things that you don't normally see. Stuff like…

• The tops of the clouds.

• The sun shining *above* the clouds.

And if you're really lucky you could get to see…
• The sunset for the SECOND time in a day. (If you take off after sunset, the sun reappears as you fly higher.)

• The shadow of the Earth. (You can see the curving shadow to the east on the tops of clouds after sunset.)

But the most amazing sensation is to have nothing under your feet. Nothing except for the plane floor and 7,000 metres of empty air.

A quick note about heights…

I hope you're not scared of heights, because there are lots of hair-raising heights and dizzying drops in this book. Here are a few to get you worried…

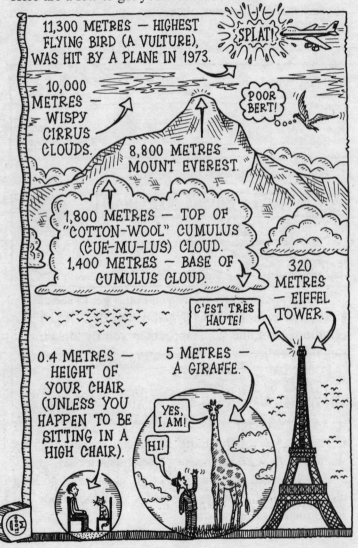

11,300 METRES — HIGHEST FLYING BIRD (A VULTURE), WAS HIT BY A PLANE IN 1973.

SPLAT!

10,000 METRES — WISPY CIRRUS CLOUDS.

POOR BERT!

8,800 METRES — MOUNT EVEREST.

1,800 METRES — TOP OF "COTTON-WOOL" CUMULUS (CUE-MU-LUS) CLOUD.
1,400 METRES — BASE OF CUMULUS CLOUD.

320 METRES — EIFFEL TOWER.

C'EST TRÈS HAUTE!

0.4 METRES — HEIGHT OF YOUR CHAIR (UNLESS YOU HAPPEN TO BE SITTING IN A HIGH CHAIR).

5 METRES — A GIRAFFE.

YES, I AM!

HI!

170

It feels scary but thrilling to fly so high. And to get this thrill, people have lost their lives and broken their legs and done terrible things to puppies and kittens. But before we get to grips with these fearsome facts, we need to find out exactly how planes fly…

A crash course in how planes fly

We've asked brainy boffins Professor N Large and Wanda Wye to build us a plane…

And now all we need is a fearless pilot to show us how it flies… Any volunteers? Well, we've just heard of a hard-up, hard-boiled, New York private eye who'll do anything for cash…

As luck would have it, MI Gutzache used to be a pilot but he quit for some reason. Anyway, he's agreed to find out how planes fly…

Er, sorry about Mr Gutzache's sickening problem. Here are the forces involved in flying…

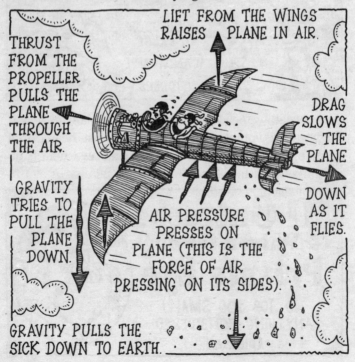

Fearsome expressions

A scientist says…

I STUDY THE SCIENCE OF DRAG

Do you say…?

MY SCIENCE LESSONS ARE A DRAG TOO!

Answer:
Say that and the scientist might drag you around his lab! Drag is the force made by air hitting something flying through the air. It affects planes and birds and underpants blowing off your teacher's washing line. And the faster the object flies, the harder drag tries to slow it down.

But what is this mysterious "lift" that raises the plane in the air? Well, in order to make sense of lift we need to know that air is made of countless tiny clumps of atoms called molecules (moll-eck-ules). They spend their time zooming about.

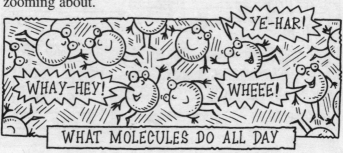

YE-HAR!

WHAY-HEY!

WHEEE!

WHAT MOLECULES DO ALL DAY

And now we can take a look at lift in action. Let's see what those air molecules are up to around the wings of Gutzache's plane…

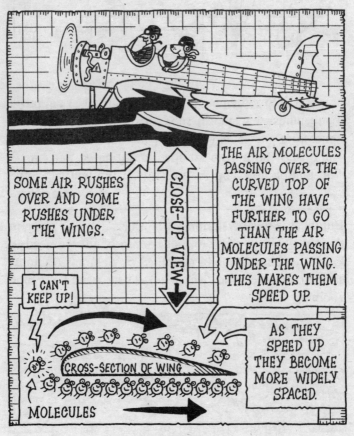

SOME AIR RUSHES OVER AND SOME RUSHES UNDER THE WINGS.

CLOSE-UP VIEW

THE AIR MOLECULES PASSING OVER THE CURVED TOP OF THE WING HAVE FURTHER TO GO THAN THE AIR MOLECULES PASSING UNDER THE WING. THIS MAKES THEM SPEED UP.

I CAN'T KEEP UP!

CROSS-SECTION OF WING

MOLECULES

AS THEY SPEED UP THEY BECOME MORE WIDELY SPACED.

The force of air pressure becomes weaker above the wing than under it. And BINGO – the air pressure under the wing lifts the wing (and the plane) higher! Yes, every plane in the world stays up with the help of tiny air molecules!

WEAKER AIR PRESSURE

CROSS-SECTION OF WING

STRONGER AIR PRESSURE

LIFT

CLEVER, EH?

Phew – did you get all that? Oh well, it's easy to remember. You get a lift in a plane and the plane gets a lift from its wings. And now for a quick quiz to "lift" your spirits…

The wing shape, curved on top and flatter underneath, is called an aerofoil. Which TWO of the following has an aerofoil shape?

a) A ski-jumper's body

PLEEEEEEASE LET IT BE ME!

b) A flying custard pie
c) A boomerang

Answer:
a) YES. Ski jumpers lean forward as they fly to make an aerofoil shape. This keeps them in the air for longer.
b) NO … and don't go chucking one at your little sister to find out.
c) YES, the aerofoil shape of the boomerang makes it glide through the air at 160 km per hour.

Bet you never knew!
Native Australians used boomerangs for hunting animals. The thin edge of the boomerang came in handy for cutting open the skins of dead animals in order to get at the tasty heart, kidneys and liver.

But of course a plane can only get lift to fly if it has wings. So can you guess what would happen if the wings fell off while the plane was flying? Well, it's just happened to MI Gutzache and Watson…

Without wings, the plane loses lift and Gutzache and Watson have to leap for their lives. Only drag slows them down as they fall – but luckily they're wearing parachutes. The parachutes open and trap billions of air molecules, massively increasing the force of drag and slowing their fall. So they have a nice soft landing…

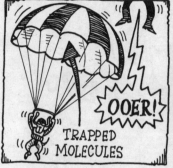

Well, that was scientifically interesting – by the way, I wonder where Gutzache's sick landed?

Now I bet you can't wait to build a plane that'll fly better than the Professor and Wanda Wye's effort – and you can on page 269. But first you'll need a bit more technical know-how, so let's start with two simple experiments…

Dare you discover … how life can be a drag?

What you need:

Two pieces of paper (but *don't* use your science homework and DEFINITELY don't tear pages from this book). The pieces of paper should be the same size.

What you do:

1 Screw up one of the pieces of paper. (I warned you *not* to use your science homework!)

2 Hold one piece of paper in each hand. Hold them as high as you can…

3 And drop them a few times…

You should notice:

The screwed-up paper ALWAYS hits the ground first. The flat sheet may see-saw or glide through the air. It falls more slowly because it has a larger surface area for billions of air molecules to push against.

Dare you discover ... how to make a flying saucer?

What you need:

A polystyrene party or picnic plate (better make sure there isn't a custard pie on it before you throw it!)

Eight 1p coins (It might be worth asking for £1 coins. They're not useful for the experiment, but they are useful for spending!)

Sticky tape

Scissors (plus a helpful adult to help with cutting)

What you do:

1 Use the sticky tape to stick the coins to the rim of the plate as shown.

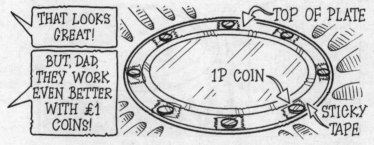

2 Practise throwing the plate upside down. (That's holding the plate upside down, NOT standing on your head!) By the way, you only need a gentle waft of your wrist to throw the plate. It doesn't work if you chuck it.

3 Throw the plate the right way up.

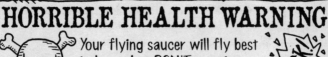

HORRIBLE HEALTH WARNING

Your flying saucer will fly best indoors, but DON'T practise throwing it near valuable china, brothers, sisters or family pets.

CRACK!

You should notice:

1 When you throw it upside down, the plate should glide smoothly through the air. If it doesn't, flick it more gently. Upside down, it forms an aerofoil shape and flies like the well-known toy called a frisbee.

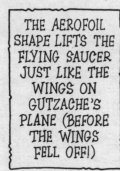

THE AEROFOIL SHAPE LIFTS THE FLYING SAUCER JUST LIKE THE WINGS ON GUTZACHE'S PLANE (BEFORE THE WINGS FELL OFF!)

WEAKER AIR PRESSURE

STRONGER AIR PRESSURE

2 When it's the right way up, the plate doesn't have an aerofoil shape and so it crashes.

THIS IS GETTING RIDICULOUS!

FLOP!

But frisbees aren't the only things that glide – birds such as seagulls glide, too (as you'll find out on page 231). Birds glide and fly so well because their wings are aerofoil shaped. And now here's a pigeon to explain how they compare to planes…

1 According to legend, in 1500 BC King Kai Kaoos of Persia was flown to China by eagles tied to his throne. The eagles were flapping after some goat's meat stuck on spears just out of reach. Sadly, when they got to China the birds guzzled the meat and the miserable monarch was stuck in the desert.

2 But that didn't stop an inventor in Baltimore, USA. In 1865 he dreamt up an eagle-powered flying machine. The eagles could be steered using cords but they might not have worked if the eagles had spotted a tasty rabbit far below...

Psst – I'll let you into a secret! These machines were as useless as a hamster in a body-building contest. In fact, all attempts to fly like a bird with flapping wings risked a messy death. Which is a bit scary, because a little bird tells me the next chapter is full of them. Oh well, at least it's got parachutes in it too!

BIG-BRAINED BIRD MEN AND PLUNGING PARACHUTES

Have you ever had a secret urge to be a bird?

Me neither – I mean, I don't even like budgie seed! But that's probably how the story of human flight began – people looking at birds and longing to soar into the sky as free as a … er, bird. And they told stories about people who could fly. Let's look at these dusty old legends…

Hmm, maybe they're a bit *too* dusty.

ESCAPE FROM CRETE

Daedalus was the greatest inventor in Greece, but he had a problem. He was stuck on the island of Crete and its mean-minded king, Minos, wasn't going to let him and his son Icarus leave.

"What more do you want, Your Majesty?" grumbled Daedalus. "I've designed a maze for your half-human, half-bull monster to live in. Now I want to go home!"

"Ha ha, you'll have to fly first," jeered the cruel king.

That gave Daedalus an idea, and secretly he built two pairs of wings from feathers and wax — one for Icarus and one for himself.

"Now, son," said Daedalus. "These wings are our ticket out of here. They've only got one problem — the wax melts easily, so don't you go flying too close to the sun."

"I won't!" promised Icarus.

One morning, before King Minos's men could stop them, the brave pair launched themselves from a cliff and flew over the sea.

"Whee! This is COOL!" laughed Icarus as he whizzed over the waves like a seagull. On and on they flew, but Icarus forgot his promise and began to soar higher and higher until he was close to the sun. The heat melted the wax, which dripped from the wings. And before Daedalus could save him, the wings fell to bits.

With a cry of horror, Icarus plunged from the sky like a sack of potatoes. AARRGGGGGGH — SPLOSH! He hit the sea far below. And that was the end of him. Daedalus made it to Greece, but he spent the rest of his days mourning his lost son. And he never flew anywhere again…

THE HAPPY HAT TRICK

Young Shun had a problem. His dad didn't like him BIG TIME and had him locked up. Shun escaped disguised as a bird, but his dreaded dad caught him. The boy escaped a second time, this time disguised as a dragon... Now, if you ask me, the guards must have been a bit dozy. I mean, wouldn't you notice if a giant goose hopped past your nose? And wouldn't you look twice if a huge scaly dragon slithered over your shoes? Anyway, Shun's dad wasn't too impressed by his son's acting ability and decided to do him in.

So he locked poor Shun in a high tower and set it on fire. Surely, thought the dastardly dad, this time I'll cook Shun's goose (and his dragon too). But Shun had one more card to play...

Seizing two big reed hats, the boy leapt fearlessly from the tower and floated harmlessly to the ground. And after that you won't be too surprised to know that Shun became Emperor of China and his dad... well, the legend doesn't say, but I hope he suffered a fearsome fate.

The reed hats were probably too small to act like parachutes and slow the boy's fall. But supposing they were extra-large hats – it's just possible that the parachute was invented in ancient China!

As for the Daedalus story, that couldn't possibly be true. But don't take my word for it – here's our pigeon pal to tell us why humans can't fly like birds…

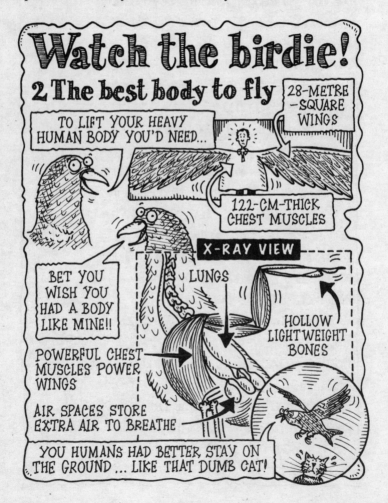

Of course, if there'd been Horrible Science books 1,000 years ago, the people you're just about to meet might have read that last bit and decided to throw away their wings. But come to think of it, they were foolish enough to jump anyway...

Four foolish fall guys

1 Bladud
Date: 863 BC
Day job: King of Britain (according to legend). Educated in Athens and founder of the first English college. (If he invented schools, he sure had it coming.)

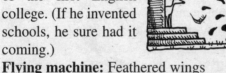

Flying machine: Feathered wings
Deadly downfall: Off the top of a temple.
Rotten result: SPLAT! Bloody for Blad.

2 Oliver of Malmesbury
Date: 1029
Day job: English monk
Flying machine: Feathered wings
Deadly downfall: Off the tower of Malmesbury Abbey.
Rotten result: Two broken legs. Oddball Ollie blamed his dangerous dive on not sticking a feathered tail on his battered bum.

3 Giovanni Battista Danti
Date: 1503
Day job:
Italian mathematician
Flying machine: Feathered wings
Deadly downfall: His first glide over a lake left him unhurt, so he celebrated by jumping off Perugia Cathedral.
Rotten result: Serious injury.

4 Marquis de Bacqueville
Date: 1742
Day job: French nobleman
Flying machine: Wings on his arms and legs
Deadly downfall: Tried to fly across the River Seine in Paris.

Rotten result: Crashed into a washerwoman's dirty old barge and broke both his legs.

The stick-insect-brained nobleman was described as…

188

And you might say that about the rest of them too – and the dozens of other tower jumpers I haven't got time to tell you about. "So what's the answer?" I hear you cry. Well, they could have tied themselves to a giant kite…

Fearsome flight fact file

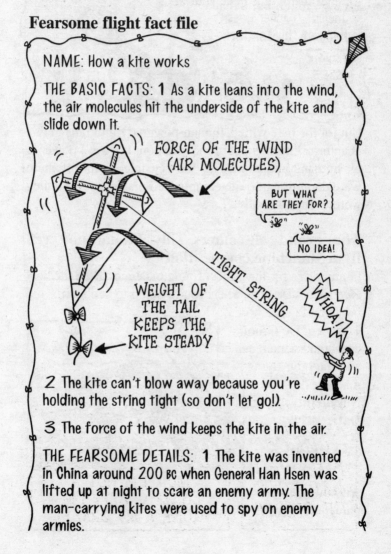

NAME: How a kite works

THE BASIC FACTS: **1** As a kite leans into the wind, the air molecules hit the underside of the kite and slide down it.

FORCE OF THE WIND (AIR MOLECULES)

BUT WHAT ARE THEY FOR?

NO IDEA!

TIGHT STRING

WHOA!

WEIGHT OF THE TAIL KEEPS THE KITE STEADY

2 The kite can't blow away because you're holding the string tight (so don't let go!).

3 The force of the wind keeps the kite in the air.

THE FEARSOME DETAILS: **1** The kite was invented in China around 200 BC when General Han Hsen was lifted up at night to scare an enemy army. The man-carrying kites were used to spy on enemy armies.

2 According to Italian traveller Marco Polo (1254–1324), stupid or drunken men were picked for this perilous job. And some men were tied to kites as a punishment. Let's hope your ancient teacher doesn't think of this torture!

WHAAAAA!

I THINK SHE'S SORRY, SIR!

But for the half-witted, human-powered flight fans in this chapter, a kite was out of the question. It wasn't powered by humans and it was far too sensible. Some of them were dreaming of quite complicated machines – and they were even more silly…

The grand all-comers silly human-powered flying-machine competition

Grand prize for the silliest flying machine – free medical care (one way or another, you're going to need it!).

1 Vincent De Groof's combined parachute and flapping flying machine
Nationality: Belgian
Date: 1874

ARRRGH!

↰ VINCENT DE GROOF GETTING IN A FLAP

Advantages: It worked the first time in Belgium as a parachute. Pity the flapping wings were useless.

Disadvantages: It didn't work in a later test over London. The frame broke and the machine was a dead loss. Sadly, De Groof was an even deader loss.

Judge's verdict: The machine isn't strong enough to fly. I'd rather bounce up and down on an exploding whoopee cushion than go up in that thing.

2 Leonardo da Vinci's flapping machine
Nationality: Italian
Date: About 1500

YES! YES! YES! YES! YES! ...NNNNNO!

THE GROUND

Advantages: It looked kind of arty in Leo's sketch book – but then he was a great artist.

Disadvantages: If anyone had built it and flown it, they would have found they didn't have enough muscle power to flap the wings.

Judge's verdict: It would make a good exercise machine.

3 Jacob Degen's flapping flying machine and balloon
Nationality: Swiss
Date: 1809

IGNORE THIS BIT!

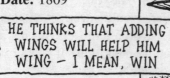

HE THINKS THAT ADDING WINGS WILL HELP HIM WING – I MEAN, WIN

Advantages: The machine hangs from a balloon, so it flies even if the wings don't work.

Disadvantages: The wings DON'T work.

Judge's verdict: Grr! This machine is a disgrace – using a balloon to fly is cheating! Degen is DISQUALIFIED and he's been suspended – er, hold on, he's already suspended from the balloon.

Bet you never knew!

In 1809 a crowd in Paris was so cross that Degen's invention wasn't a proper flying machine that they chased dodgy Degen out of town.

4 Dr WO Ayre's pedal-powered propeller thingie

Nationality: USA

Date: 1885

CARDBOARD CLOUDS FOR ADDED EFFECT

Advantages: It would make a great kiddie's climbing frame or even a bedstead. You had to pedal very hard to pump the tubes full of air that in turn powered the propellers – so it kept you fit.

Disadvantages: Everyone laughed at you.

Judge's verdict: The propellers would never get enough power to lift anything heavier than a hamster. But it's a worthy RUNNER-UP in our competition. It's almost silly enough to win … but not quite!

5 Jean Pierre Blanchard's sail- and pedal-powered flapping machine
Nationality: French
Date: 1781

PREPARE FOR TAKEOFF!

Advantages: Included a musician to play soothing music so you wouldn't get scared. Guaranteed 100 per cent safe. (It's too heavy to leave the ground!)

Disadvantages: See advantages. Especially the bit about not flying.

Judge's verdict: THE WINNER! Easily the most freaky flying machine ever – and it's even got in-flight entertainment!

GOLDEN BRICK AWARD

ZANK YOU!

Human-powered flight sounds a fatal flop, doesn't it? And so it was … until the 1970s when scientists built a human-powered flying machine that flew. But a lot of things happened in the story of flight before then, so you'll have to hang on until page 299 to find out what happened. And no peeping!

In the meantime, the tower jumpers continued their deadly dives and the machine makers continued to create crazy contraptions. And the only reason more weren't killed was because their wings sometimes worked like Shun's hats – as parachutes. Pity they didn't work for poor de Groof.

Obviously the parachute is a vital bit of kit for every fearless flier – but who invented it? Well, experts argue about it until they're blue in the face and the question is a bit of a hot potato...

WHO INVENTED THE PARACHUTE?

The fearsome fight to parachute

1485 Leonardo da Vinci designs a parachute but doesn't test it – any volunteers?

1779 Joseph Montgolfier makes a parachute and tests it by dropping a sheep from a tower. The sheep lands safely – now that's what I call a woolly jumper.

1785 Our pal Jean Pierre Blanchard experiments by tying a puppy to a parachute and dropping it from a balloon. (Don't try this at home.) The pup was fine, but as you'll find out on page 211, Blanchard was DOG-ged by misfortune.

1808 The parachute saves its first life when Polish balloonist Jordaki Kuparento makes a hasty exit when his balloon catches fire.

But early parachutes weren't all they were cracked up to be – and sometimes they did crack up. And my deeply dodgy mate, Honest Bob, wants to sell you some. Er, you'd best be warned – you may want to take what he tells you with a pinch of salt ... or even a few tonnes of salt.

A couple of facts that Honest Bob left out...

1 Garnerin's parachute swayed a lot in the wind. Each time he tried it he swayed until he was sick – but at least he lived, unlike...

2 Robert Cocking. "I never felt more comfortable," declared the 61-year-old artist just before falling to his death when the parachute broke.

What's that? You feel your teacher or puppy or brother or sister would enjoy a parachute jump? You haven't asked them, but you feel sure they'd like the idea once they were plunging through the air...? Well, I think it's a good idea to find out how they might get on...

Dare you discover ... how to make your teacher try a parachute jump?

What you need:
Ruler
Biro and paper
Scissors (and the same helpful adult who helped with the cutting in the previous experiment – hopefully they weren't injured too badly)
Paper napkin (about 32 x 32 cm)
Blu-tack
Thread
Sticky tape
Paperclip

What you do:
1 Cut a piece of paper 4.5 cm long and 2 cm wide. Fold it as shown and draw your teacher on both sides.
2 Cut an 80-cm length of thread. Fold it in half lengthways and cut again to make two 40-cm lengths.
3 Thread one length of thread through the paperclip. Stick the ends of the threads to the napkin as shown.

4 Repeat step three with the second length of thread.

5 Make sure the paperclip is halfway along the lengths of thread and use a tiny blob of Blu-tack to stick the threads to the paperclip.

6 Place the napkin on the table so that the paperclip is underneath. Cut 7-cm corners off the napkin as shown.

7 Add the sticky tape as shown. Tuck the ends of the tape under the edges of the napkin.

8 Gently use the point of a biro to make a hole 0.5 cm across at the centre of the sticky-tape cross.

9 Slide the paper with your teacher's picture into the paperclip.

10 Now for the fun bit. Drop your teacher from a height! No, I didn't mean your real teacher!

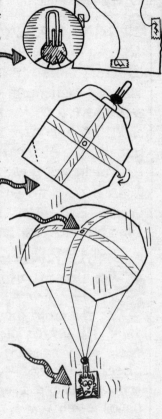

You should find:
The parachute swings from side to side just like Garnerin's bucket chute. This happens because air trapped under the parachute tries to escape, pushing it from side to side. The hole lets air escape and stops the parachute from swaying too much – and that's why modern parachutes have holes in their tops...

197

OK, so you've found out how a parachute works – but how does it *feel* to make a jump? A US Air Corps scientist named Harry Armstrong made a jump and asked himself this very queasy question. Here's my version of his notes…

MY PARACHUTE JUMP
by Harry Armstrong

So here I am in the plane. I feel a mixture of fear and excitement - well, fear mostly. I really should have gone to the toilet when I had the chance. Oddly enough, I'm so scared that I can't hear the plane's engine. It is still working, isn't it? I'm trembling with nerves - please forgive the shaky writing.

TREMBLE!

OK, this is it - I'm at 670 metres. I'm about to jump … wish me luck!

ARRRGGGGGGGGGGGGH! I'm tumbling head over heels at 190 Km per hour (please forgive the even more shaky handwriting). I think I'd better close my eyes. Oh — that feels oddly relaxing — I think I'll Keep them closed … Hmm — but what if I hit the ground before I open my eyes? YIKES! I could even wake up to find myself dead! Hmm, I'd best open my eyes. I'm at 579 metres and the ground is coming up to meet me. Er, hello, ground! Now where's my parachute rip cord? Oh no, that's my shoelace…

TUG!

And you'll be cheering out loud to hear that Harry landed safely. But the girl in our next story didn't look set for a happy landing. I've got three excuses to tell this terrible true tale…

a) It's exciting.

b) It was the first time anyone used a parachute to rescue another person.

c) It features a flying machine that you can find out about in the next crazy chapter.

The Daily News
1908

DARING DOLLY SAVES MAY'S DAY!
~

Daring parachute stunt jumper Dolly Shepherd and her friend Louie May faced certain death yesterday. As the girls dangled from an unmanned balloon 7,000 metres in the air, luckless Louie couldn't free her chute.

Daring Dolly (whose previous jobs include being a waitress and a target for a blindfolded sharp-shooter) bravely battled to free her friend.

When Louie was freed, the two girls jumped using Dolly's parachute. But they fell too fast and Dolly hurt her back. Said Dolly from her bed, "It gave me a nasty jolt – especially the landing. Ouch! My poor back! Where's me vapour rub?"

Dolly Shepherd

199

But you'll be jumping with joy to read that, four years later, Dolly realized that too many scary stunts would kill her, so she gave up parachuting. And she lived to the ripe old age of 97.

So, did you spot the flying machine we'll be talking about next? No? Huh! Well, here are a few more clues: it's big and round and filled with hot air or gas (which sometimes leaks). It can be dangerous...

NO! It's a balloon – so read on. The next chapter will take you to new heights...

BARMY BALLNS

Balloons are a pretty sight as they sail silently through the skies – but the fight to fly them was far from pretty. We're about to take to the air with a curious crew of brilliantly barmy balloonists and be swept away on a gale of fearsome facts… Er, do you think this chapter's actually *safe*?

The fearsome fight for balloon flight

1670 Italian priest Francesco de Lana hits on a nifty plan. Get some really light air from high up in the sky and fill hollow copper balls with it to lift a flying machine. So how do you get this air (that no one is sure exists)? Er, build a flying machine. And how do you do that when you haven't got the air yet…?

THAT'S WHERE MY PLAN FALLS DOWN…

1709 Brazilian priest Laurenço de Gusmão shows the King of Portugal a model hot-air balloon complete with fire. The fire spreads to the royal palace. The fire is put out, but oddly enough His Majesty isn't put out, despite nearly ending up as a roasted royal.

1755 French priest Joseph Galien (and by the way, why is it that priests were barmy about balloons?) suggested a de Lana-style flying machine 1 km long. His bosses tell him to take a nice long holiday. Now that's a holy order I could live with…

Meanwhile, a pair of brothers who weren't actually priests were about to make a brilliant, if barmy, breakthrough…

A puff of smoke

We last saw Joseph Montgolfier (1740–1810) chucking an unfortunate sheep from the top of a tower. But that was just a harmless hobby – the real business of Joe and brother Jacques (1745–1799) was making paper. I expect they were quite rich … on paper. One day in 1782, Joseph watched sparks floating up his chimney – well, there wasn't too much on telly as it hadn't been invented yet.

Joe saw that hot gases from the fire were lifting the sparks, so he decided to fill a paper bag with hot air to test whether that would rise. His landlady suggested a silk bag as it would be less likely to burn, and they watched as the bag sailed up to the ceiling. (By the way, don't go lighting fires in your house to make bags rise up – this is not a sensible thing to do, unless you'd enjoy eating prison food until you're no longer a menace to society.)

Anyway, Joe's experiments led to models that got bigger and flew higher until...

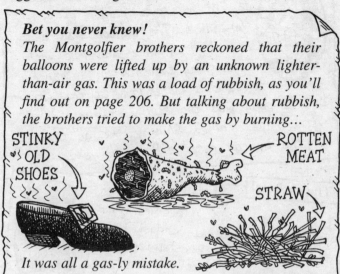

Bet you never knew!
The Montgolfier brothers reckoned that their balloons were lifted up by an unknown lighter-than-air gas. This was a load of rubbish, as you'll find out on page 206. But talking about rubbish, the brothers tried to make the gas by burning...

STINKY OLD SHOES

ROTTEN MEAT

STRAW

It was all a gas-ly mistake.

But the Montgolfiers were scenting success (and lots of other smelly things). And at last they were able to launch the first flight with an air crew in the history of the world.

AND WE'RE THE COCK-A-DOODLE-CREW!

Yes, the first living beings to fly in a flying machine were farmyard animals! And now, in a Horrible Science World Exclusive, the animals quack, bleat and crow for themselves, with a little help from King Louis XVI of France...

The King

14 September 1783 was a great day at my royal palace of Versailles. The balloon was a huge ball of blue and gold with a cage slung beneath it. I wanted to take a close look at the fire but le pong was too stinky. Pfwoar! What were they burning? Anyway, we all cheered as the balloon rose high in the sky.

The cockerel

Yes, it was a great day for us fowls - the first time we've flown without wings! Yes, it certainly was a booster for this rooster! Pity the woolly-minded sheep had to kick me as we landed in a forest 3.2 km away.

The sheep

Baah! That stupid rooster kept pecking at my legs the whole time. I'm not one to bleat, but I reckon he was scared chicken!

The duck

I'm just a duck - so what do I know? But personally I think they're all quackers. I mean, if they want to fly, why don't they just flap their wings? It works for me!

204

Barmy balloon quickie quiz

1 How were the Montgolfier brothers rewarded by the King?

a) They were given a cake in the shape of a balloon.

b) They were given a gold medal.

c) They were locked up in prison and forced to sniff smelly socks for making nasty whiffs in the palace.

2 How was the sheep rewarded?

a) It was made into a rather tasty mutton stew.

b) Its wool was made into an itchy pair of royal underpants.

c) It was given a home in the royal zoo.

Answers:
1 b)
2 c) And that was a good deal nicer than King Louis' fate. He had his head chopped off in 1793.

Bet you never knew!
Scientist Jean-François Pilâtre de Rozier (1757–1785) and the Marquis d'Arlandes volunteered to fly in the Montgolfiers' balloon. The flight was a soaraway success, although they did set the balloon on fire and had to put it out using wet sponges. And they spent the flight arguing because the Marquis was too busy admiring the view to put straw on the smelly fire.

Meanwhile, French scientists were feeling mightily miffed because the balloon breakthrough had been made by a pair of papermakers and not a superb scientist. So the French Academy of Sciences asked Jacques Charles

(1746–1823) to invent a scientific flying machine. And he did – the hydrogen balloon. So what happened next? Did Charles's balloon rise to the occasion or did he go down like a lead – er – balloon?

Well, before we find out, let's look into how balloons work – it's sure to be a gas but it's nothing to sniff at! It's all to do with density…

Fearsome expressions

A scientist says…

YOU'RE TOO DENSE TO FLY…

Do you say…?

I'M QUITE BRAINY, ACTUALLY.

Answer:
Say that and the scientist really will think you're dense stupid. The scientist means your body weighs more than an equal volume of air – so it's too heavy to fly.

But here's a really cool thought…

Just imagine that your body was *less* dense than air. If your body weighed less than 5 grams, the weight of a sugar lump, you could actually float in the air! Instead of swimming pools there'd be air pools, and instead of high dives there'd be sky dives! You'd feel light-hearted as you walked on air … unless you sat on a pin and you went pop, or the gas escaped from you like a balloon with its neck open and you flew around making rude noises.

Anyway, when a balloon is full of hydrogen gas or hot air, it's less dense than the surrounding air. And that means it can rise like a bottom-burp bubble in a bath…

Here's a modern hot-air balloon…

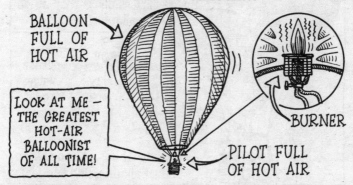

BALLOON FULL OF HOT AIR

LOOK AT ME – THE GREATEST HOT-AIR BALLOONIST OF ALL TIME!

BURNER

PILOT FULL OF HOT AIR

Air is heated by the burner. Heat gives the air molecules more energy so they travel faster and further. They push against the sides of the balloon, filling them out.

IT'S GREAT TO BE WARM!

YEAH, LET'S RUSH AROUND!

To bring the balloon down, you simply switch off the burner. The air cools and takes up less room. More cool air can enter the base of the balloon and as it becomes heavier it dips down. Simple, innit?

And now for the hydrogen balloon…

The hydrogen balloon is a bit more complicated but, as luck would have it, we're about to see one in action.

After the embarrassing near-fatal failure of their plane, Professor N Large and Wanda Wye have built a balloon. And MI Gutzache's been paid loads of money to fly it…

Balloon is full of hydrogen gas. The gas is less dense than air so the balloon rises up.

Gas-release valve (to let gas escape)

PULL!

Ballast (bags of sand) stop the balloon rising too fast.

GOOD LUCK, GUTZACHE!

By throwing out ballast, Gutzache makes the balloon lighter. This makes it rise…

OOPS!

OOOF!

By opening the valve, Gutzache reduces the balloon's lifting power, so it should come down…

TUG!

GRR — THE VALVE'S STUCK!

Later that night…

I CAN'T SEE A DARNED THING… LUCKY I BROUGHT SOME MATCHES

No, Gutzache! Hydrogen burns easily when mixed with air…

Oh dear. Is our hero a grilled Gutzache? Is Watson a hot dog? All will be revealed on page 262. But now back to Jacques Charles, who is still busily inventing the hydrogen balloon…

> **Bet you never knew!**
> *A number of scientists hit on the idea of using hydrogen in a balloon before Charles, but they couldn't think of anything to put the gas in. Scottish scientist Joseph Black planned to fill a body bit from a dead calf with the gas, but he never got round to it. Maybe he was a bit of a cow-ed.*

In fact, Charles's hydrogen balloon hid a silky secret…

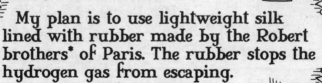

TOP-SECRET PLAN
by Jacques Charles
Not to be read by anyone –
especially not those
bungling, jumped-up
Montgolfier brothers…

J.C.

My plan is to use lightweight silk lined with rubber made by the Robert brothers* of Paris. The rubber stops the hydrogen gas from escaping.

* Yes, more brothers!

Thousands of people turned up to see the balloon launch and the scientist put his invention under armed guard to keep the crowds away. Sadly, the guards weren't around when the unmanned balloon landed near a village and a gang of scared peasants and their dog ripped it to bits. It must have been an un-peasant surprise for the annoyed inventor.

On 12 December Charles and his friend Noel Robert took off from Paris in another balloon. An even bigger crowd came to wave them off. Overcome with emotion, Charles exclaimed...

Which was true – the trouble was the sky was also rather cold. After a flight of 43 km, Robert got out. The lightened balloon rose 2,743 metres and chilly Charles nearly froze to death. But he did get to be the first man ever to see the sun set twice in one day...

By now, all Europe was balloon barmy and what better challenge for fledgling fliers than to fly the English

Channel between France and Britain? The race was on, and by June 1784 Englishman James Sadler and Frenchman Pilâtre de Rozier were planning to make the trip. But first to start was Jean Pierre Blanchard... Now I know they didn't have radio in those days, but if they had, I bet the flight would have been broadcast live and it might have sounded like this... (Why not get a friend to read this bit aloud? You can close your eyes and imagine you were there!)

Life is full of ups and downs

Hello and welcome to Dover... My name's Mike Commentator... As I speak, brave balloonist Jean Pierre Blanchard and his passenger Dr John Jeffries are about to fly the Channel. But all is not well. We've heard that the two fliers had a row after Blanchard was caught wearing a weight-belt. The sneaky sky-sailor planned to pretend the balloon was too heavy for Jeffries – and grab all the glory for himself!

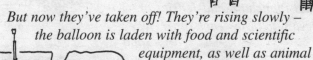

But now they've taken off! They're rising slowly – the balloon is laden with food and scientific equipment, as well as animal bladders to help it float if it lands in the sea. They've even got the world's first airmail letter...

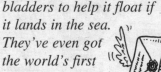

OH NO! Blanchard's let too much gas out of the balloon. They're coming down in the sea. They're throwing things out to lighten the balloon. Out goes food, drink and scientific equipment. And now Blanchard's chucked out the useless oars and propeller he brought to control the balloon. Will the balloonists escape a ducking?

CHUCK!

FLING!

YES! They're going up – but will they make it? NO, they're coming down again! And now it looks like they're arguing! Oh my goodness, they're taking off their clothes! Yes, Blanchard's just dropped his trousers. They're down to their underwear and things are looking desperate – they've even thrown away their bottle of brandy. But they're still coming down. They're just about to hit the sea and Blanchard and Jeffries are trying to throw each other over

GET OUT!

GRRR!

the side! Is it all over? NO! They're rising up again. THIS IS INCREDIBLE – they're going to make it! What a goal! Now that's what I call an up-and-under

HOORAY!

YIPPEE!

– or is it an up-and-down-and-over? Oh no, they're coming down in a forest – they could hit the trees! Don't look at this disgusting sight – they're weeing in the bladders and dropping them over the sides. Let's hope they don't plop on any passing peasants! Well, that was a relief – they've just missed the forest. And they've landed! The crowd are going potty and the balloonists are parading about in their pants! It looks like a potty pants party! And now back to the studio!

And so the world's first airmail letter got through to Paris. But you'll be heartbroken to hear that Blanchard died of a heart attack in his balloon in 1809.

Barmy balloonists

There's something about ballooning that brings out the barmy side of the most sensible person. And as for silly people, well, they can turn barkingly barmy. The quiz you're about to tackle is based on a very barmy balloonist...

The adventures of Loopy Lunardi

The characters:

GEORGE BIGGIN — A LARGE GENTLEMAN, IN FACT A BIT OF A BIG 'UN

VINCENT'S PETS

VINCENT LUNARDI — AN ITALIAN BALLOONIST

1 Lunardi had promised to give Biggin a ride in his balloon. But the big man was too heavy. Lunardi preferred to carry his pet cat, dog and pigeon … and what else?

a) Lots of food and wine.

b) His collection of science books.

2 During the flight everyone wanted to watch Lunardi – what was the result?

a) He killed a woman and saved a criminal's life.

b) 22,000 people visited the doctor's with stiff necks.

LET US IN, DOC – DON'T BE A PAIN IN THE NECK!

3 During the flight Lunardi's cat got cold. What did he do to help it?

a) He fed the pigeon to the cat.

b) He landed the cat in a field … and flew off.

Bet you never knew!

The next year George Biggin and his even bigger friend Letitia Sage forced Lunardi to let them fly. Mrs Sage started scoffing Lunardi's lunch and squashed his scientific equipment with a jangling crash. A few hours later they landed in a bean field. Local children thought it was a great excuse to skip lessons, but everyone got chased by a furious farmer for trampling his beans.

And if you think that sounds barmy, you ain't read nothing yet. French balloonists started doing really barmy publicity stunts. For example, in 1817 a Monsieur Mergot flew over Paris in a balloon … while sitting on the back of a white stag named Coco.

But balloons had a darker side – these things were DANGEROUS with a capital "D"!

Gruesome gas bags – 1

Even after Blanchard beat him to it, Pilâtre de Rozier still wanted to fly the Channel. Trouble is, he wanted to do it in a combined hot-air and hydrogen balloon – and remember what happens when you mix fire and hydrogen? When the balloon burst into flames, the scientist and his co-pilot were the first people to die in an air crash. And in honour of the event the bloody scene was painted for some rather sick souvenirs. Sick bags, anyone?

Gruesome gas bags – 2

Meanwhile, other scientists were dreaming of taking a balloon as high as they could to find out how the air changed with height. But this turned out to be *incredibly* dangerous. Read on, this next bit's a "height" for sore eyes…

Fearsome flight fact file

NAME: How air changes with height

MOLECULES

THE BASIC FACTS: **1** The higher you go, the more spaced-out the air molecules are. The air is said to be "thin".

2 The air is too thin to provide lift for a bird's wing. In 1862 scientist James Glaisher (1809–1903) dropped a pigeon from a balloon at a great height. The poor pigeon plummeted like a stone.

3 The temperature can be well below freezing.

THE FEARSOME DETAILS:
1 Pioneer balloonists suffered from frostbite and their hands turned black. The air was too thin to breathe easily and they often blacked out.

I DIDN'T KNOW YOU'D BROUGHT GLOVES...

NEITHER DID I!

LACK OF HAIR

GASP!

LACK OF AIR

2 In 1875 top French balloonist Gaston Tissandier and two scientists blacked out at 7,600 metres. By the time Tissandier woke up, the two scientists had died from lack of air.

Another danger with taking a hydrogen balloon to a great height is that the balloon can explode. Because the air is thinner, the air pressure is weaker on the sides of the balloon. This allows the hydrogen inside to push out with greater force and burst the balloon. And that's what happened to this fearless flier...

FAMOUS FEARLESS FLIER FILES

Name: John Wise (1808–1879)

Nationality: American

Got into flying by: Trying lots of horrible flight experiments. For example:
- He tied a kitten to a kite and flew it.
- He dropped a cat tied to a parachute from a window.

The animals lived but John's neighbours banned him from trying any more cruel experiments, so he decided to make a hot-air balloon. But it crashed on his neighbour's roof and set it on fire.

High point: Invented the rip panel. You pull it to let the gas out of your balloon if the wind is blowing it along the ground.

Low point: In 1859 he was flying with some friends when he went to sleep under a leaky gas valve. He nearly died from breathing hydrogen gas, but luckily his friends woke him because he was snoring.

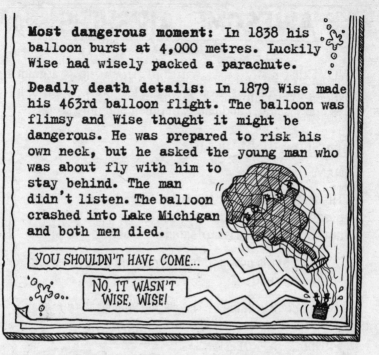

Most dangerous moment: In 1838 his balloon burst at 4,000 metres. Luckily Wise had wisely packed a parachute.

Deadly death details: In 1879 Wise made his 463rd balloon flight. The balloon was flimsy and Wise thought it might be dangerous. He was prepared to risk his own neck, but he asked the young man who was about fly with him to stay behind. The man didn't listen. The balloon crashed into Lake Michigan and both men died.

YOU SHOULDN'T HAVE COME...

NO, IT WASN'T WISE, WISE!

Got the message? Balloons are horribly hard to fly and easy to crash, and even today they're only safe in the hands of experts. But in the 1850s, flight fans thought they'd invented a superb solution...

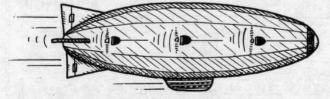

ARRGGGGH! Am I seeing things or did a huge cigar-shaped balloon just drift across the page? Oh well, you'd best read on. Reading is believing...

AWESOME AIRSHIPS

WOW, that really *was* an airship! An airship is a giant balloon that you can steer – so let's steer our way through this crazy chapter and check out their stunning secrets…

Fearsome flight fact file

NAME: Airships

THE BASIC FACTS: **1** An airship is made from several gas bags inside a tough wooden or metal skeleton. The outside of the ship is protected by a fabric or metal skin.

2 The craft is powered by engines and propellers, and steered by rudders.

3 The pointy shape of the airship enables it to move with less drag than a balloon.

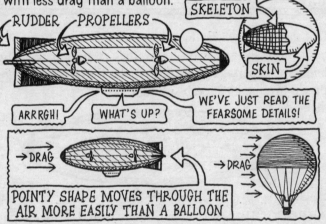

RUDDER   PROPELLERS   SKELETON   SKIN

ARRRGH!   WHAT'S UP?   WE'VE JUST READ THE FEARSOME DETAILS!

→DRAG   →DRAG

POINTY SHAPE MOVES THROUGH THE AIR MORE EASILY THAN A BALLOON

THE FEARSOME DETAILS: Until the 1930s, airships were filled with hydrogen gas, which, as you know, burns rather easily. So guess what happened in awesome airship crashes?

The fearsome fight for airship flight

1852 Frenchman Henri Gifford (1825–1882) adds a small engine to a cigar-shaped balloon. The engine is too weak to power the balloon and the craft gets blown backwards.

1883 Gaston Tissandier (remember him from page 217?) and his brother Albert experiment with a 4.8 km per hour motor. The airship flies as fast as a granny shuffles to the shops. Well, almost.

1898 Brazilian genius Albert Santos-Dumont builds his first airship and learns how to fly it. Awesome Albert is so immensely interesting that you can read all about him on page 222.

1900 Retired General Ferdinand von Zeppelin (1838–1917) builds his first airship or zeppelin. (I wonder where the name came from?)

1915 Zeppelins bomb Britain in the First World War. The Brits panic until they realize the big slow zeppelins are easy to shoot down. And then the Germans' panic and stop zeppelin raids.

1924 A zeppelin flies the Atlantic. In the 1930s zeppelins are the poshest way to travel the world.

1930 The British airship R101 crashes, killing 48 people. The Brits give up on airships.

1937 The *Hindenburg*, the biggest zeppelin ever built, crashes in the USA. Suddenly the balloon bubble bursts for airships.

So airships were as dangerous as a dinner date with a dinosaur, and one man who knew this more than most was Albert Santos-Dumont. Let's go and meet him right now…

FAMOUS FEARLESS FLIER FILES

Name: Albert Santos-Dumont (1873–1932)

Nationality: Brazilian

Got into flying by: Having an incredibly rich coffee-maker for a dad. That meant he was wealthy enough to build and fly airships for fun.

And when he wasn't flying he was racing cars. He once tested an airship engine by putting it on a tricycle and entering a car race and beating the leaders!

High point: In October 1901 Santos-Dumont tried to win a 100,000-franc prize for flying from St Cloud on the outskirts of Paris, rounding the Eiffel Tower and returning to St Cloud in half an hour. He did it with seconds to spare.

"Have I won the prize?" Santos-Dumont called.

YES! YES! YES!

roared the crazy, cheering crowd.

"No", muttered a grumpy judge from the Paris Aero Club. The fearless flier hadn't lowered his guide rope in time. At this point the rich businessman who had offered the prize said that he had won — it was either that or face a riot. Albert gave the money away to the poor.

Low point: Following his triumph, Santos-Dumont toured Britain and the USA, but his airships were damaged by vandals.

Most dangerous moment: In his bid to win the prize, Santos-Dumont suffered many hair-raising crashes. For example his first airship folded over in mid-air. He said later...

FOR A MOMENT I WAS IN THE PRESENCE OF DEATH

But just as the craft crashed downwards, he saw two boys flying a kite. The falling flier shouted to them to grab his airship guide rope and run with it against the wind. The ship gained some lift from the wind and made a soft landing.

Deadly death details: Oddly enough Santos-Dumont wasn't killed in a crash — but be warned, it's NOT a happy ending! Make sure you've got a box of paper hankies handy...

Awesome Albert's downfall

In the 1900s Albert Santos-Dumont was the most famous flier in the world. Well, come to think of it, he was the ONLY flier in the world.

In fact he even helped the first-ever child to fly in a powered flying machine. One day in 1903 the brave Brazilian landed in a children's fair. All the kids begged for a ride and all their spoil-sport parents said…

But seven-year-old Clarkson Potter pestered his parents so hard they gave in. In the end, though, he only went up a few metres.

But after planes became popular Albert didn't do so well. Although he was the first person to fly a powered plane in Europe, his planes always seemed to crash. As he grew older many people thought he was mad. He spent time in mental hospitals and dreamt of making a pair of wings and flying from a window. Quite unfairly, he blamed himself for the way planes had been used to kill people in war. One day Santos-Dumont was staying in a hotel in Sao Paolo, Brazil. Civil war was raging and the ageing flyer spotted a plane dropping bombs.

"What have I done?" he muttered.

He went up to his room and took his own life.

Zero hour for the zeppelins

By the time Santos-Dumont died, a lot had changed in the floating world of airships. Zeppelins were the world's number-one airships but things were about to go fearsomely wrong...

HORRIBLE HOLIDAYS PRESENT

Come fly on the Hindenburg!

It's got everything you've ever wanted and a lot of things you don't.

● Your very own cabin.

● Hot and cold water.

● Air conditioning.

It's a gas!

● Library, lounge (complete with piano) and bar.

● On-board pastry chef bakes fresh buns every day!

● Guaranteed smooth flight so you can munch your buns and enjoy the view with none of that nasty air sickness.

THE SMALL PRINT
The hydrogen gas and chemicals used to stiffen the fabric sides of the craft have turned the Hindenburg into a flying bomb. Have you written your will yet?

OOER!

On 6 May 1937 the *Hindenburg* was just coming into dock at Lakehurst, New Jersey... Suddenly a flame appeared that rapidly swallowed up the ship. The great airship crashed to the ground amid the screams of its unlucky passengers. Forty people died, the *Hindenburg* was destroyed ... and it all took just 34 seconds.

That was bad enough. But a cine-camera recorded the explosive event and a local radio reporter recorded it. The world got the message – airships were awesomely unsafe.

But were they? Even in 1937 it was possible to use the safer gas helium instead of hydrogen. Airships needn't burn. What killed off the airship in the end wasn't safety fears – it was the success of a nippy little rival with two wings and a whizzy propeller. And in the next chapter we'll find out how it got off the ground... Get ready to spin that propeller!

THE WRIGHT WAY TO INVENT THE PLANE

So how does anyone invent the plane? Well there's a bit more to it than sitting on the toilet and getting inspired and shouting "Eureka!" In fact, inventing is HARDER than chewing a concrete toffee. In this cruel chapter we'll find out why the Wright brothers got it Wright and why nearly everyone else ended up grumpy, wet … or dead.

Fearsome flying flops

Back in Victorian times lots of inventors dreamt of making a flying machine. Trouble is, most of them had little idea of the forces that affect flight, and their planes were as useless as a giraffe with a sore throat. But that won't stop Honest Bob trying to sell you one. YOU HAVE BEEN WARNED!

HONEST BOB'S PLANE PRODUCTS PRESENTS...

"My Bob's really musical. When he was little he was always on the fiddle." Bob's mum

HERE ARE SOME CLASSIC PLANES YOU'LL BE FLYING TO DIE, I MEAN, DYING TO FLY...

I Fancy a trip to Beijing? Henson and Stringfellow's steam-powered plane will get you there! Finest 1840s technology!

ARE WE REALLY FLYING?

Only £99,999.05p – but I'll knock off the 5p for cash.

NO, IT'S JUST AN ADVERT!

227

2 You'll be batty not to buy this bat-winged plane (1890) by Clement Ader. People say it's an objet d'art - although it looks more like a paper dart to me.

Only £150,000 plus a few hidden extras.

HE'S WAVING GOODBYE, MUM!

DON'T GET TOO EXCITED

3 Get fired up to the MAX-im with Hiram Maxim's monster plane (1894). Yeah, this plane's the business - I mean, old Maxim invented the machine gun and a mousetrap, so I bet he knew all about planes. Look, I'll even throw in a free Maxim mousetrap and cheese if you buy it.

PREPARE TO TAKE OFF...

... ALL THE HEAVY STUFF THAT'S STOPPING THIS CONTRAPTION FROM FLYING!

Price £299,999.99.
Buy now or regret it later!

4 You'll be Venetian blind not to buy it! (Well, it looks like a Venetian blind!) Horatio Phillips's multi-wingy thingie (1904). I mean, talk about character – this plane's got it in spades. If it doesn't take off, you can always put it in your window and it'll keep the sun out.

OH WELL, I'LL USE IT AS A CAR!

STILL ON THE GROUND

Price £199,999. Unless I'm in a good mood – then it's £299,999.

A few facts that Bob was going to tell you some day...
1 The designers thought plane 1 would fly to China, but it was too heavy to fly at all.
2 Plane 2 hopped in 1890, but that was all.
3 Plane 3 hopped slightly in the air and broke the rail it was running on.
4 According to its inventor, plane 4 hopped 152 metres – yeah, right. Mind you, old Horatio was one of the first people to realize the importance of aerofoil wings. He just made rather too many of them...

Meanwhile, other flight fans were being a little more thoughtful. They wanted to understand about flight before trying to build a plane, so they studied birds, and built and flew gliders and learnt to fly them. These people included the Wright brothers, but before we pay them a visit we really ought to glide over a few facts...

Fearsome flight fact file

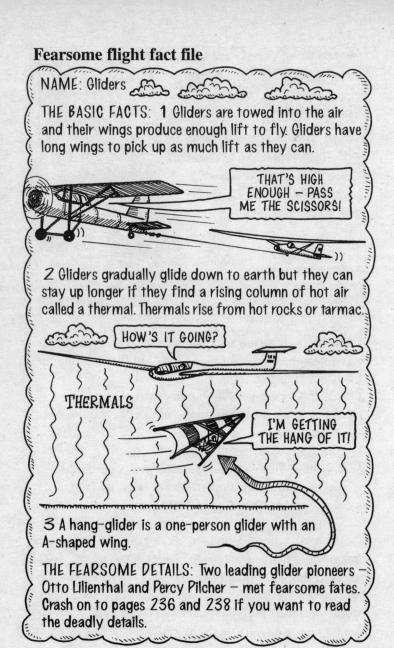

NAME: Gliders

THE BASIC FACTS: **1** Gliders are towed into the air and their wings produce enough lift to fly. Gliders have long wings to pick up as much lift as they can.

THAT'S HIGH ENOUGH — PASS ME THE SCISSORS!

2 Gliders gradually glide down to earth but they can stay up longer if they find a rising column of hot air called a thermal. Thermals rise from hot rocks or tarmac.

HOW'S IT GOING?

THERMALS

I'M GETTING THE HANG OF IT!

3 A hang-glider is a one-person glider with an A-shaped wing.

THE FEARSOME DETAILS: Two leading glider pioneers — Otto Lilienthal and Percy Pilcher — met fearsome fates. Crash on to pages 236 and 238 if you want to read the deadly details.

Not surprisingly, the cleverest bloke in this book was keen to study how birds flew. And that's how he came to build the world's first glider…

Hall of fame: Sir George Cayley (1771–1857) Nationality: British
Young George was just 12 years old when he heard about the Montgolfier brothers' amazing balloon, and he

became flight-mad. He started making his own hot-air balloons powered by candles (very dangerous, so don't try it). And then he experimented with model helicopters made of feathers. As he liked to boast...

I HAVE IDEAS, LOTS OF IDEAS THAT MAY BE MADE TO WORK.

And so he had! In a lifetime of spare-time study (he was a busy landowner and politician), Cayley worked out...
- The ideal shape for a plane.
- The ideal shape for a wing.
- The importance of the forces of lift and thrust.
- The sort of controls a plane would need.

Here's an experiment which shows clever Cayley at his best. Eager to find out the angle of a wing that gives the most lift, he made a model wing based on the wing of a dead crow. He spun the model on a whirling arm powered by a weight that he dropped downstairs and found that an angle of 45° was best. Now that's what I call a stair-lift. By the way, cunning Cayley had to weight, er wait, for his wife to be away as she didn't approve of him experimenting in the house.

And here's how Cayley built his glider...
Cayley built his first model glider in 1799 and flew it as a kite – but he didn't get round to building a full-sized glider for ten years, and he didn't test one with a human on board for another *thirty* years! As I said, George was *very* busy.

In 1849 Cayley finally tested his glider with a person on board. That person was a ten-year-old boy and he flew a few metres. The boy was the first person to have flown in a glider and you might think the lucky lad became incredibly famous and sold his story to the newspapers for pots of money. But no – science is horribly unfair and no one even noted the boy's name!

Four years later, Cayley built a machine that could carry an adult. Once again there are few records of this world-shattering event, but Cayley's ten-year-old granddaughter saw the whole thing and here's how she might have described it...

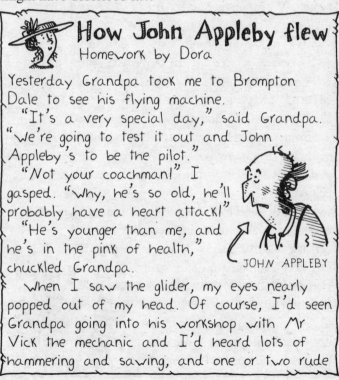

How John Appleby flew
Homework by Dora

Yesterday Grandpa took me to Brompton Dale to see his flying machine.

"It's a very special day," said Grandpa. "We're going to test it out and John Appleby's to be the pilot."

"Not your coachman!" I gasped. "Why, he's so old, he'll probably have a heart attack!"

"He's younger than me, and he's in the pink of health," chuckled Grandpa.

JOHN APPLEBY

When I saw the glider, my eyes nearly popped out of my head. Of course, I'd seen Grandpa going into his workshop with Mr Vick the mechanic and I'd heard lots of hammering and sawing, and one or two rude words when they hammered their fingers. But I'd never dreamt of anything like this...

downhill

Proudly Grandpa showed off his creation. He pointed out the rudder at the rear to help Mr Appleby steer the craft and the elevators on the wings to help it go higher.

"All my own inventions," Grandpa beamed.

By now a crowd of villagers had gathered to watch the takeoff and some of the men offered to pull the rope on the front of the craft to get it going.

John Appleby was sitting in the craft, wearing his warmest coat - but I noticed he didn't look quite as jolly and red-faced as usual.

"You'll be fine, Appleby," smiled Grandpa, cheerfully slapping his coachman on the back.

John Appleby gulped and nodded. I bet he was thinking what would happen if the glider crashed and he broke all his bones and his brains came out of his ears.

SPLURB!

With a signal from Grandpa, the men started pulling on the ropes. Harder and harder they pulled. The glider slid over the grass and bounced downhill and then...

Everyone gasped as it took off. It flew like a paper dart over the stream and across the valley and... OH NO! It bashed into the other side of the valley in a big cloud of dust. I felt disappointed - I thought Grandpa's glider would fly much further. Everyone rushed over to see if John Appleby was all right. Was he dead?

No. Mr Appleby was coughing and spluttering and spitting out dust. He leapt from the glider as if it was a boiling-hot bath. His chins were wobbling, his face was the colour of cold porridge and his whiskers were sticking up like a wire brush.

"SIR GEORGE," he yelled, "I WISH TO GIVE NOTICE. I WAS HIRED TO DRIVE AND NOT FLY!"

"Don't worry, Grandpa!" I cried. "I'll fly the glider if John Appleby won't."

"Oh no, you don't!" snapped Grandpa. "It's far too dangerous for girls!"

"Oh well," I hear you remark, "at least John Appleby became world-famous..." But he didn't. In fact, the newspapers didn't even report the story. Most people thought that making a plane was impossible and they couldn't see the point of Sir George's experiments. You see, no one had invented an engine that was light and powerful enough to get a plane in the air.

Bet you never knew!
1 The steam-powered engines of Cayley's day were very heavy and needed boilers to make steam. Not to mention a supply of water to boil and coal to burn.
2 Cayley realized this made it impossible for a plane to fly and planned to build a gunpowder-powered engine ... before he realized it was too dangerous.

MAYBE NOT!

So, for now, the future of flight depended on building better gliders and that's exactly what flying freaks tried to do. The most famous of them all was a German genius who didn't mind making the odd sacrifice…

FAMOUS FEARLESS FLIER FILES
Name: Otto Lilienthal (1849–1896)
Nationality: German
Got into flying by: Watching storks fly as a child. He became

an engineer but he retired to build gliders.

High point: Gliding several hundred metres at heights of 30 metres. Lilienthal was the first human in history to glide like a bird and he made 2,000 glides — some from a specially built hill. Today the modern sport of hang-gliding is inspired by his work.

WEEEEEE!

Low point: Trying to build a flying machine with flapping wings. Experts say it wouldn't have got off the ground.

Most dangerous moment: Just about every moment he was in the air. Lilienthal's gliders were built out of wood and fabric, and they were hard to control in windy weather. To change course, he had to swing his body from side to side.

Deadly death details: Luckless Lil was trying to turn in a wind. He fell and broke his back and his final words were, "Sacrifices must be made." In other words, he was dying for flying.

Oddly enough, Lilienthal's famous fate did nothing to put people off gliding. It even seemed to encourage them!

Bet you never knew!
The US champion gliding geek was another ex-engineer named Octave Chanute (1832–1910). Chanute was a little too old to fly so he asked a man named Augustus Herring to test his gliders. (When the glider didn't work too well, I bet he lost his temper and turned into a red Herring.)

In Britain, Lilienthal's lead was taken up by Percy Pilcher (1867–1899). Percy had worked for Hiram Maxim (remember him from page 228?), but he became a fan of Lilienthal and even flew with his hero. And, like Lilienthal, he was to die in a glider crash.

FLYING NEWS
1899

PERCY PILCHER PERISHES!

Flying freak Percy Pilcher perished after a gliding glitch caused a cruel crash. Penniless Percy invited some bigwigs to watch the takeoff of his new powered plane. But bad weather and engine trouble caused his hopes to take a nosedive. Plucky Percy decided to show off his glider even though it was soaked by the rain. The glider fell to bits and Percy's fall proved fully fatal.

Bet you never knew!
Experts think that, with a couple of tweaks, Percy's plane might have flown. So thanks to a spot of engine bother and rotten weather, Percy missed out on flying the world's first powered plane. Sadly, instead of tasting the high life he ended up biting the dust.

And talking about powered planes, it's time for some very exciting news for anyone who gets excited by engines…

Exciting engine news

The reason why Percy could build a powered plane was that a new kind of engine had been developed. Let's face the facts – this new engine was vital for the fearsome future of flight...

Fearsome flight fact file

NAME: The very vital petrol engine

THE BASIC FACTS:
1 The petrol engine was invented in 1883 by German Gottlieb Daimler (1835–1900).

2 It was vital for planes because it was powerful enough to power plane propellers and provide the thrust they need to fly but was light enough not to weigh the plane down.

SUPER-LIGHT POWER GENERATING INVENTION!

1 PETROL AND AIR SQUIRTS INTO CYLINDER

2 SPARK SETS FIRE TO FUEL

BOOM!

CYLINDER

PISTON

4 PISTON IS SUCKED UPWARDS PUSHING OUT WASTE GASES

3 EXPLOSION PUSHES PISTON DOWN WHICH TURNS THE SHAFT

SHAFT

THE FEARSOME DETAILS: The only problem was that petrol burns easily – with fiery results in plane crashes.

And it was the petrol engine that made it possible for a pair of bicycle mechanics from Ohio, USA, to make the world's first-ever powered flight. Back in 1899 no one had ever heard of them (except maybe their mum), but armed with a few bike spares, cloth and some bits of wood they would change the history of the world...

Everything you ever wanted to know about the Wright brothers

When Orville Wright (1871–1948) and his brother Wilbur (1867–1912) were little, their dad gave them a toy helicopter powered by a rubber band. They loved it so much they broke it. They built a new one but their grumpy, spoilsport teacher took it away.

Just think about it! That teacher set back the tide of human progress by years and it's worth sharing this idea with your teacher next time they seize your pocket computer game. And you can always get your revenge by torturing them with this terrible test...

WARNING! These questions are rated really hard, if not impossible. They are only suitable for teachers and NOT friends. If you are feeling kind, you can give your teacher the right to ask the class to vote on the answer to ONE question.

Terrible teacher torture test

1 Who was the unsung star who helped the Wrights with their work and never got any glory?

a) Their sister.

b) Their pet fly Francis.

c) Their teacher.

2 What did Wilbur and Orville do as a hobby?

a) They printed a newspaper.

b) They entered custard-pie throwing competitions.

c) They gave lessons to local children.

3 What did Wilbur do when a boy sat on his best hat?

a) He made the boy test a dangerous glider.

b) Nothing at all.

c) He gave the boy loads of horribly hard homework.

I WOULDN'T HAVE MINDED... BUT I WAS WEARING IT!

4 The Wrights tried to fly at Kill Devil Sandhill near Kitty Hawk, North Carolina. Why?

a) The sand gave them a nice soft landing when they crashed.

b) The wind blows all the time.

c) Their old teacher lived there.

5 Where did a bit of the Wrights' plane end up?

a) Holding up their mum's washing line.

b) The moon.

c) On display at their old school.

THIS IS ONE SMALL STEP FOR MAN... HANG ON, WHAT'S THIS?

Answers:

1 a) So let's hear three cheers for Katharine Wright, who ran the bike business when the boys were off inventing the plane. She gave them the cash they needed to get off the ground.

2 a) But the really interesting thing is that the inventive brothers actually built their own printing press from an old tombstone and the top of a pram (plus other bits 'n' pieces).

3 b) This story shows how patient Wilbur was. You could try to explain that patience with children is a sign of genius – but would your teacher be patient enough to listen?

4 Ha ha – trick question. The answer is **a)** AND **b)** and your teacher can't have a point unless they said both. In fact the wind wasn't as constant as the brothers hoped, and millions of mosquitoes sucked their blood. But at least there was no one around to spy on them and pinch their ideas. (The Wrights were keen to keep their invention a secret until they could make money from it.)

5 b) When the Apollo 11 astronauts landed on the moon in 1969 there was a bit of the Wrights' plane in their spacecraft. Well, you didn't think it flew there on its own, did you?

What your teacher's score means...

5 CHEAT! Clearly this person is unfit to be a teacher!

3–4 Good. Make sure the questions are harder next time.

0–2 Poor. Make your teacher write out 1,000 times "I really ought to know more about the Wright brothers" while you take the day off.

By the way, the **c)** answers were to do with school, so if your teacher's answers were all **c)** they are clearly overworked and deserve a long holiday. And you'll have to take one too!

The Wrights get busy...

From 1899 onwards the Wright brothers spent all their spare time building and testing gliders and planes until they had built a plane that could fly. And that's not all...

• They invented a lighter and more powerful petrol engine.

• Plus a new, more powerful propeller.

• They built a wind tunnel (that's a machine in which air is blown through a box) to work out which aerofoil wing shape gave the most lift.

• But, best of all, they realized that it wasn't enough to build a plane. They had to be able to control it in the air. And so they invented wing-warping, which means flexing the wings to alter the amount of lift they provide. By doing this the Wrights could tilt and turn the plane in mid-air.

And they did all this by trial and error – testing, testing and testing their designs until they worked. In all, they tested...

• Hundreds of aerofoil shapes in their wind tunnel.

• Their third glider nearly 1,000 times.

Although they didn't know it at the time, the Wrights were in a race to invent the plane. And their rival was scenting success. His name was Samuel P Langley (1834–1906) and he was an astronomer who got hooked on flying after going to a scientific talk. Now I could tell you more about Langley, but it so happens he's coming back from the dead to tell you himself. He's on the TV show that digs the dirt to unearth its guests...

Welcome to Dead Brainy — the programme where we give dead scientists the time of their lives, er, deaths.

Tonight's guest is Samuel Langley.

GOOD EVENING.

You're looking grave, Sam.

WELL, THAT'S WHERE I'VE BEEN SINCE 1906.

So tell us about your plane...

IT COST THOUSANDS OF DOLLARS AND IT WAS LAUNCHED FROM A GIANT CATAPULT ON TOP OF A BOAT.

So is it true everyone you worked with had to dress smartly and wasn't allowed to swear?

WHY AREN'T YOU WEARING A TIE?

244

And what's more, we're getting ahead of our story. After all, back in 1903, when Langley's plane flopped in the river, the Wrights' plane, the *Flyer*, wasn't a flyer. It hadn't even got off the ground.

And to tell the story of what happened, let's peek at Orville Wright's secret diary. Er, I bought it from Honest Bob, so it *might* be a forgery.

Orville Wright's Secret Diary

December 16 1903, Kitty Hawk, North Carolina. It's all my brother's fault. Two days ago he tried to take off but the controls were set wrong and he crashed. Ever since, we have been repairing the damage and waiting for the wind to drop so we can risk trying to fly again. Time is running out and we've got to be home for Christmas or Pa will never forgive us!

GRR, WHERE ARE THEY?

December 17 1903
We decided to fly this morning. To be honest, there's been times when I've doubted we'd do it. It's taken four years of hard work. Would it all be worth it? I wondered. I asked a local named John Daniels to take a photo if the plane flew - but John hadn't used a camera and he didn't know which end was which. Slowly, we pushed the plane from its shed. John and his friends helped.

CAN I GO FIRST, BRUV?

NO WAY!

I lay on the lower wing (that's where the pilot has to go - we really ought to invent a comfy seat!). As Wilbur swung the propeller to start the engine, the others pushed the plane along our home-made rails. The engine coughed and spluttered into life... WHOOSH! My heart jumped into my mouth. I was up in the air. I WAS FLYING! At last the plane came down but I'd done it. The flight was awesome, it was MASSIVE, it was all of 40 metres - and I must have been in the air for a WHOLE 12 SECONDS. WOW!

I CAN DO BETTER THAN THAT!

And it just got better. John Daniels did manage to take my photo - pity I wasn't smiling at the time! And after coffee Wilbur flew 52 metres - huh, trust my brother to try to beat me! So I showed him - I flew 61 metres, although I did go up and down a bit. But just when I felt like crowing, my big-headed brother flew 100 metres, although he did crash. Luckily he's fine - what's with him always crashing? Then it was my go and I beat his record, but then he flew for nearly a minute and got 260 metres. Show-off!

We sent a telegram to Pa telling him we'd be home for Christmas. Now that's what I call a GOOD day's work!

ANYBODY WANT A WING?

And so, after years of trying, humans were flying powered planes. But many people thought it was no big deal. After all, the Wrights had flown for less than a minute and the only papers that reported the event got it all wrong and said Wilbur ran around shouting "Eureka!"

But from now on the fearsome fight wasn't to fly. It was to fly *better*! And the race was on to build better planes…

PLANE-CRAZY PLANES

This is a chapter about machines. Flying machines and not-so-flying machines. It's got the sort of machines that you wouldn't send your worst teacher up in, and it's even got helicopters too. So, if you're all aboard, let's take to the air…

Now I bet you're itching to find out what happened to the Wright brothers, who were last seen celebrating their success with a slap-up Christmas dinner. The Wrights knew they had to improve their plane before they could think of selling it and making money. So they built not one but two planes, *Flyers* 2 and 3. And they tested the planes until they could…

• Fly 66 km.
• Reach the dizzy height of 110 metres.

At last, in 1908, the brothers set out to wow the world and sell planes. Orville went to Washington to wow the US army. And Wilbur went to Paris to wow European flying fans.

At first the French didn't think much of Wilbur. They didn't like his greasy old clothes and the way he slept in a plane shed and ate from tins and burped in public. But once they saw what his plane could do, they changed their tune…

LE SCRUFFBALL! LE SLOB!

LE SUPERSTAR!

After all, the best the Europeans could manage was a giant box-kite, which our old pal Santos-Dumont managed to hop 4.5 metres off the ground: not even as far as Wilbur's best 1903 effort.

So when the Europeans saw Wilbur flying happily across country and changing course in mid-air, they were gobsmacked. They rushed to their own garden sheds and started knocking up all kinds of crazy craft based on the Wrights' planes. But tragedy was just around the corner…

The Wrights' planes were FEARSOMELY dangerous fliers:
• They had NO brakes.
• No undercarriage wheels.
• No safely belt.
• The only way women could fly in them was with their legs tied together so their dresses wouldn't blow over their heads.

In 1908 Orville was flying over a cemetery in Washington when he lost control. He was badly hurt and his passenger Thomas Selfridge was killed. The aeroplane had claimed its first victim…

Bet you never knew!

1 Despite the safety problems, the Wrights made plane-loads of money from selling their planes. But they hated other pilots stealing their ideas and they spent years in the courts fighting their rivals. Wilbur ruined his health with worry. In 1912 he died of a grisly gut disease.

2 The Europeans didn't copy everything from the Wrights. They began to use wing flaps called ailerons (a-ler-rons) instead of wing warping. Ailerons proved ideal for tilting wings to turn a plane in mid-air (see page 164 for the full flap facts).

But talking about dangerous machines … here's Honest Bob with a collection of perilous planes. Yes, they're more dangerous than a tiger with toothache, so which one would you fancy for your death-day, er, birthday?

HONEST BOB'S PLANE PRODUCTS PRESENTS…

"My Bob loves nature – his favourite animal is the cheater." Bob's mum

PLANES TO DIE FOR!
YOU GET TO FLY AND I MAKE A KILLING!

1 The Christmas Bullet (1918) This ye olde antique plane was designed by Dr William Christmas, so it makes an ideal Christmas present. Dr C was a medical doc and I bet that came in handy when his plane crashed. It goes like a bullet and it's twice as deadly. (Oops, I'm getting a bit too honest!) Price – it's only £999,999.99.

ERR... I'LL BE IN A WOODEN BOX BY BOXING DAY!

2 The Mayfly (1910) Built in Ireland by Lilian Bland, the Mayfly is held together with piano wire. A must for music lovers! The engine was made from Lil's aunt's ear trumpet and an old whisky bottle.

WHEN THEY ASKED ME, I SAID, "IT **MAY FLY** ... AND IT MAY NOT!"

Price – it's yours for 50p (plus £654,321 postage and packing).

3 Le Grand (1913) What a grand way to fly! You get a crew of three – one person to fly the plane, one to sit at the front and tell the pilot what they see, and one to walk backwards and forwards to balance the plane. Relax on the supplied-as-standard comfy four armchairs and sofa! Price - you can't put a price on this kind of luxury but I'll try - it's £2,222,222.22.

A BIT TOO COMFY!

ZZZZZ ZZZZZ ZZZZ

ZZZZZ ZZZZ

4 Count Gianni Capriani di Taliedo's seaplane* (1921) You can count on this superb seaplane (probably). I mean, it's got nine wings and eight engines so it doesn't matter if a few drop off! Price - if you give me £10,000,000, I'll tell you!

WELL, IT FLOATS!

BUT DOES IT FLY?

* A seaplane is a plane that's designed to take off and land on water. For this reason seaplanes have skis rather than wheels underneath. Yes, they're water-skiing planes!

5 The Granville Gee Bee (GB Sportster) (1930s) OK, so it's a bit dangerous and it might just give you the heebie-jeebies - but it flies at 470 km per hour and it adds spice to your death, er, life. This plane makes a real deep hole when it crashes - so it saves getting buried! Price — name your price, and I'll just add £456,789!

...BETTER HEAD FOR THAT GRAVEYARD

6 The Flying Flea (Pou de Ciel) (1930s)

Supplied as a kit — you build this plane yourself in your shed. Yeah, it's ideal for DIE fans, er, I mean DIY fans. It's cheap and cheerful, and it even flies upside down. Well, it does that most of the time.
Price — just 50p.
Glue: £89,000.
Come to think of it, you can just fly it away — if you dare!

YIKES! I'VE BEEN ITCHING TO FLY ONE BUT IT'S NOT UP TO SCRATCH!

Six things Honest Bob forgot to tell you about these planes

1 The Christmas Bullet was a killer craft. On its first flight, its wings fell off and its pilot was killed. On the third test flight, another pilot died. Dr C was a flying fibber who stole many of his inventions from other companies.

2 Lilian's Mayfly didn't fly – it hopped. Her uncle was so scared that he offered her a car if she never flew again.

3 In 1913 Le Grand was the biggest plane in the world and the first with a cabin. Despite, or because of, all its pilots, the plane designed by Russian genius Igor Sikorsky (1889–1972) actually flew!

4 The good news – this plane took off from Lake Meggidore. The bad news – its middle wings fell off and it crashed. Everyone had a good laugh ... except the plane-ly annoyed Count.

5 The Gee Bee was built for racing and actually set a speed record. It also had a nasty habit of killing its pilots. Two Gee Bees crashed and killed their pilots. So the makers put bits of the two downed planes together to make a third Gee Bee – which crashed and killed its pilot. For some reason this put people off flying it.

6 In the 1930s there was a craze in France, Britain and the USA for these home-built planes designed by Henri Mignet. Mad Mignet had been plane-crazy since he built a glider that landed on his little sister. He said:

IF YOU CAN NAIL TOGETHER A PACKING CRATE YOU CAN CONSTRUCT AN AEROPLANE

Trouble was, when the Flea flopped upside down, you couldn't get it the right way up until you crashed and died (probably).

An important announcement by the author...

So far, all the planes in this chapter have been dismal embarrassing flops, but there *were* good planes in the 1920s and 1930s... Between 1919 and 1931 the Schneider Trophy seaplane races encouraged designers in the USA, Germany, Italy, Britain and France to build faster planes. The designs inspired fighter planes, like the British Spitfire and the Italian Maachi C200.

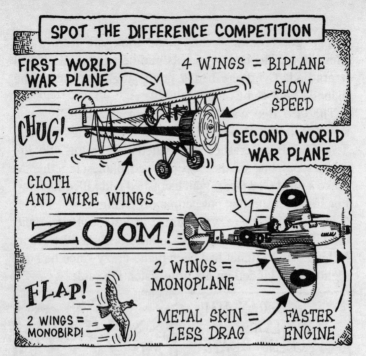

SPOT THE DIFFERENCE COMPETITION

FIRST WORLD WAR PLANE

4 WINGS = BIPLANE

SLOW SPEED

CHUG!

SECOND WORLD WAR PLANE

CLOTH AND WIRE WINGS

ZOOM!

FLAP!

2 WINGS = MONOPLANE

2 WINGS = MONOBIRD!

METAL SKIN = LESS DRAG

FASTER ENGINE

Horrible helicopters

And that wasn't all. In the 1930s designers were working on a totally new type of flying machine. A machine that took off and hovered without bother. Or at least it was supposed to…

Five facts that your teacher probably doesn't know about helicopters

1 The helicopter was invented in ancient China. Or at least a toy helicopter that whizzed up in the air when you pulled a string was invented there. It reached Europe in the Middle Ages.

2 Before 1900 loads of people tried to invent the helicopter, including Leonardo da Vinci. But, as with planes, there were no powerful engines that could make them fly. In 1877, for example, French inventor Emmanuel Dieuaid tried to solve the problem by putting a steam boiler on the ground to feed a steam engine on a helicopter. But the craft couldn't fly higher than the steam pipe. So I guess it was all a pipe dream.

3 In the 1880s US inventor Thomas Edison (1847–1931) tried to solve the problem with a helicopter engine powered by explosive gun cotton. But then his lab blew up. Edison was a bright spark but he didn't need that sort of spark.

4 In the 1900s inventors began to get off the ground in their helicopters – but not more than a few metres.

5 The first really useful helicopters were inspired by Spanish inventor Juan de la Cieva, who invented the idea of a spinning rotor on top of a flying craft. By the end of the 1930s German inventor Heinrich Focke and Igor Sikorsky (yes, the guy who brought us *Le Grand*) had built their own helicopters.

Bet you never knew!
Helicopter pilots have silly slang terms for their machines. It's worth learning them so you can impress your friends by pretending to be a helicopter pilot...

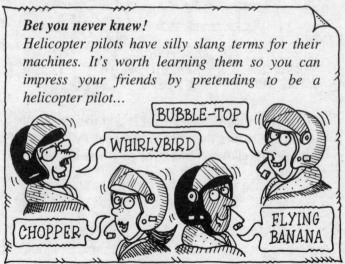

But if you really want to be a helicopter pilot, you need to know how they work – or even how to build one yourself...

Fearsome flight fact file

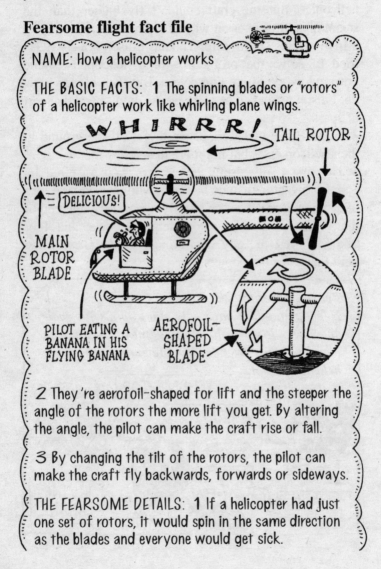

NAME: How a helicopter works

THE BASIC FACTS: **1** The spinning blades or "rotors" of a helicopter work like whirling plane wings.

WHIRRR!

TAIL ROTOR

DELICIOUS!

MAIN ROTOR BLADE

PILOT EATING A BANANA IN HIS FLYING BANANA

AEROFOIL-SHAPED BLADE

2 They're aerofoil-shaped for lift and the steeper the angle of the rotors the more lift you get. By altering the angle, the pilot can make the craft rise or fall.

3 By changing the tilt of the rotors, the pilot can make the craft fly backwards, forwards or sideways.

THE FEARSOME DETAILS: **1** If a helicopter had just one set of rotors, it would spin in the same direction as the blades and everyone would get sick.

258

2 That's why most helicopters have a second set. They push the tail round in the opposite direction to the spin of the main rotors. Oh well, it saves on sick bags.

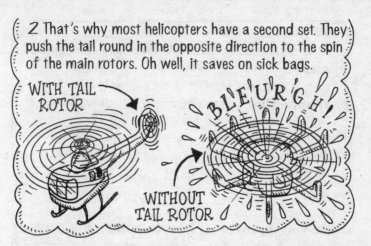

WITH TAIL ROTOR

BLEURGH!

WITHOUT TAIL ROTOR

Watch the birdie!

4 Hummingbirds and helicopters

WE HUMMINGBIRDS CAN HOVER...

UNLIKE ROTORS, OUR WINGS BEAT BACKWARDS AND FORWARDS IN A FIGURE OF EIGHT... UP TO 70 TIMES A SECOND!

OUR LONG BEAK IS HANDY FOR DRINKING NECTAR FROM FLOWERS.

I NEED A STRAW!

Hmm – I expect the burgers would be chargrilled and, all in all, I guess it's safer to build a helicopter than to try to be one...

Dare you discover ... how to build a helicopter?

A QUICK NOTE TO OVER-EXCITED YOUNGER READERS

NO, it's not a real helicopter and you shouldn't try flying in it. You'll have to carry on pestering your parents if you want a real chopper for your birthday.

What you need:
Piece of paper 21 cm by 9 cm.
Ruler
Scissors (and that ever-helpful adult helper)
Paperclip
Pencil

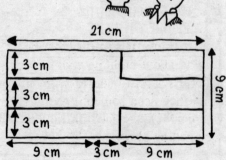

HERE WE GO AGAIN

What you do:
1 Draw the solid lines on the paper as shown.

21 cm

3 cm
3 cm
3 cm

9 cm

9 cm   3 cm   9 cm

260

2 Cut the paper along the solid lines.

3 Fold the paper along the dotted lines as shown. These folded bits are your rotors.

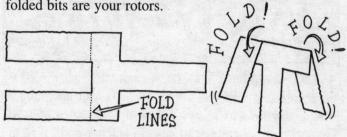

FOLD LINES

4 Now open up your rotors and slide the paperclip over the bottom end of your helicopter.

STAND BY...
FIVE, FOUR,
THREE, TWO,
ONE...

5 Ready for your first flight? Simply drop it from a height!

You should find:
The rotors spin – just like the blades of a real helicopter.

An important announcement...

Talking about building flying machines, I've just heard that our scientist buddies have built another plane. Once again they need someone to put it through its paces. So where's MI Gutzache? Oh, silly me – I forgot, he was last seen getting blown up.

KABOOM!

As luck would have it, Gutzache and Watson escaped by parachute and were only a bit singed. And now, as I'm sure you'd love to know how to fly, we've offered MI Gutzache a vast amount of cash to teach Wanda Wye his flying skills…

MI GUTZACHE'S FLYING SCHOOL LOG-BOOK

Flying lessons, they said. Nice and simple – no balloons, no blasts. "Yeah, right," I said – that's what I always say and, as always, I was right. But the balloon had blown up my wallet and I needed the cash. I played a hunch and I took the job. Would I be the fall guy again? I wondered. Time would tell – but just then time wasn't letting on.

LESSON I WEAR THE RIGHT CLOTHES

It's cold up there, I wear…

FLYING HELMET

GOGGLES

RIDICULOUS MOUSTACHE

SCARF TO STOP ME GETTING STIFF NECK

GOOD LUCK, WANDA!

WATERPROOF FLYING SUIT

THERMAL UNDERWEAR (UNDER JUMPERS)

TWO WOOLLY JUMPERS (UNDER SUIT)

SEVERAL PAIRS OF WOOLLY SOCKS

Things to take...

HOT-WATER BOTTLE

THERMOS AND SANDWICHES

VOMSAK SICK BAG

LUCKY CHARM

PARACHUTE - I AIN'T GOING UP WITHOUT ONE!

LESSON 2 KNOW YOUR PLANE

You've got to control the plane, or else you crash. But to do that you need to know your way around the machine...

8 PROPELLER

7 ENGINE

OK, HERE'S WHAT YOU NEED TO KNOW

1 TAIL

4 RUDDER

2 TAIL PLANE

9 FLAPS

6 AILERON

3 ELEVATOR (ONE ON EACH TAIL PLANE)

5 WING

263

And here's what they do...

1 Tail stops the plane sliding from side to side.

2 Tail plane provides lift for the tail.

3 Elevators are used to take off, climb and dive.

4 Rudder steers the plane right or left.

5 Wings provide lift and keep the plane flying level.

6 Ailerons tilt the wings.

7 Engine powers the propeller.

8 As the propeller speeds up, it pushes air past it to produce thrust and pull the plane forwards.

9 Flaps increase drag and slow down the plane for landing.

LESSON 3 CONTROLS

It feels good to get your hands on the controls, but don't do nothing stupid with them in the air or we'll be kitty meat.

● The control column moves the ailerons and elevators.
● The brakes slow the plane down on the ground.
● The pedals move the rudder.

KITTY SNAX

- The compass shows your direction.
- The throttle controls the engine speed.
- The speedometer shows your speed.
- The altimeter shows your height.

CONTROL COLUMN

PILOT SEAT

THROTTLE

PEDALS

LESSON 4 TAKEOFF AND LANDING

Before you take off it's a smart idea to check out your plane. Make sure the wings are stuck on, etc. Then check your instruments and make sure they work. Now have I forgotten anything? Nope!

Switch on the engine. Get a good buddy to swing your prop - that's what we pilots call turning the propeller to get it started. Taxi along the runway, open up the throttle to power up the engine - try NOT to run down the Professor and that stupid darn cat!

When you're going fast enough, pull up the control column to raise the elevators. This boosts the lift over the tail - so it rises up.

CHEERS, PROF!

WE'RE FLYING!

MEOW!

RUN FOR IT, TIDDLES!

To land, slow the engine and push the control column forward to lower the elevators and reduce lift. Don't forget to brake your wheels after you land!

LESSON 5 STEERING THE PLANE

You can steer the plane using the rudder pedals: left for left and right - well, you get the picture. But if you do just this, the plane skids about in the sky...

OOER!

So it makes sense to bank the plane. "Bank"... I love that word - it reminds me of wads of cash. Up here it means tilting the wings and steering the rudder at the same time. So to bank right, it's control column right and right rudder pedal down...

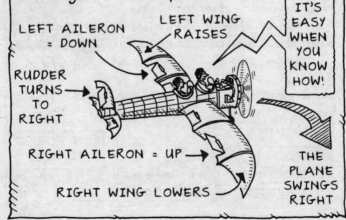

LEFT AILERON = DOWN

LEFT WING RAISES

IT'S EASY WHEN YOU KNOW HOW!

RUDDER TURNS TO RIGHT

RIGHT AILERON = UP →

RIGHT WING LOWERS

THE PLANE SWINGS RIGHT

So you'd like to learn to fly, too? Well, don't let me stop you!

Dare you discover … how to bank a plane?

What you need:

Yourself

That's it. (No, you don't need a plane – I bet you're not old enough to fly one anyway, are you?)

What you do:

1 Place your arms out straight like wings. Make sure your hands are facing down and your wings are pointing slightly upwards and well away from your granny's glass goblet collection or your dad's chin.

2 Your hands are your ailerons. Practise using them…

a) Tilt your right hand so your little finger is higher than your thumb.
b) Tilt your left hand so your thumb is higher than your little finger.
3 Now you've raised your right aileron, your right wing (arm) should lower. And because you've lowered your left aileron, your left wing (arm) should raise. This means you can bank to the right.
4 Now try banking left.

NEEEEEEEEEEE EEEEOOOOWW WWWWWW!

You should find:

You get the hang of the controls quite quickly. Now try running around as you practise banking complete with sound effects. Just don't try it at family mealtimes … or in posh china shops.

Oh, so now you want your very own plane to practise flying in? Well, here's one that's safer than a Flying Flea and less grisly than a Gee Bee…

Dare you discover … how to build a world-beating plane?

> This plane was inspired by Ralph Barnaby's winning entry in the 1967 Great International Paper Airplane competition.

What you need:
An A4 piece of paper

💀 HORRIBLE HEALTH WARNING
Do NOT use family photos or your little brother's homework for this job. Soggy toilet paper is also STRICTLY banned.

A table (it helps to do the folding on a hard surface).
Scissors (ask your local friendly adult to do the cutting).

What you do:
1 Fold the paper lengthways. Make sure the fold is nice and sharp.
2 Draw this shape and cut it out.
3 Now draw this line using a ruler. Use the ruler to make sure the line joins up with the bottom left corner.
4 Fold along the dotted line as shown.

5 Fold the front edge of the plane up as shown and then fold it twice more, as if you were rolling up a carpet.
6 Fold up the ends of the wings as shown.

7 Throw the plane *gently*. But don't absent-mindedly throw it at your brother or sister, overhead power line, priceless family heirlooms or the dog.

8 Now cut an aileron on each wing, like so…
9 And an elevator on each half of the tail, like so…
10 Try throwing your plane with the controls set in different ways.

You should find:
The ailerons and elevators work just like the plane Gutzache was flying on page 266. Well, a bit better actually.

Mind you, it doesn't matter how well your plane flies – it's not going anywhere without someone to fly it. Someone brave and fearless who doesn't mind risking their neck. In the early days of flight, pilots had to be barmy or brave to fly at all … but are you brave enough to read about them?

POTTY PIONEER PILOTS

OK, so it was a bad idea to throw a pioneer pilots' party. The wacko wing-nuts are showing off and swinging from the light fittings and doing handstands on the windowsills. But then I guess if you risk your life to fly it helps if you're a little loopy…

Bet you never knew!
In 1922, star US pilot Jimmy Doolittle did handstands on a windowsill at a party in Chile. He fell, breaking both his ankles – but that didn't stop him putting on an awesome air display a few days later.

Anyway, we've got to make our excuses and dash off for France in 1909, where a pair of fearless fliers are about to race for glory … or death.

Time for a Channel chase (again!)

Inspired by the sight of Wilbur Wright flying with ease, the European flying freaks began to build better planes and set their sights on a new goal. Just as in the early days of ballooning, the race was on to fly the English Channel and win £10,000 from a British newspaper. Here are the front runners – who do you fancy to win?

DATE	Name: LOUIS BLÉRIOT	Name: HERBERT LATHAM
1906	I'm a rich car headlamp maker.	I'm a rich thrill-seeker.
1908	I've spent all my money building planes that crash.	I've got a deadly lung disease. I don't mind if I die!
1909	If I don't win the prize, I'll be ruined!	I'm going to fly the Channel - or die!
19 JULY	Wait! I'm not ready yet! 	Grr - I tried to fly but I crashed into the sea! 
23 JULY	I've burnt my foot! I can't sleep!	Wake me up at 3.30 am to fly!
24 JULY 3.30 am	Time to go!	Zzzzzzzz.
4.50 am	OH NO, I'm lost and my engine's overheating! Phew! It's raining. That'll cool it down.	Grr - why didn't you wake me up? Now it's too late to catch Blériot!

5·10 am

HURRAH — I've won! I've arrived in England!

Good morning!

GRRRR — I'VE LOST!

Bet you never knew!
1 Blériot was cheered by a crowd as he landed. And then he was questioned by a miserable customs official, who thought he was a smuggler.
2 The future held very different fortunes for our two fearless fliers. Blériot made another fortune as a plane maker – everyone wanted to buy his channel-flying plane, the Blériot XI. Latham went big-game hunting and got gored to death by a charging buffalo.

THIS IS ONE CHARGE I CAN'T AFFORD!

The race across the Channel wasn't the only risky race around. In 1911 a US newspaper boss offered $50,000 to the first pilot to fly across the USA in 30 days. Pilot Calbraith Rodgers tried to win the prize, but on the way he suffered...

- 16 crashes.
- Including five really BIG crashes.
- And used enough spare parts to build *four* planes.

His worst crash was just 19 km from the sea. He wrecked his plane, spent weeks in hospital with a broken leg and didn't win the prize. The next year he went back to the area and crashed after smacking into a seagull. Rodgers died and the seagull probably hopped the twig too.

But even without the perils of racing, pilots were crashing and dying in fearsome numbers. In just one year, 1910, 37 pilots were killed in crashes. And that was a fair proportion of all the people who could fly at the time!

Four ways to nearly kill yourself if you're an early flier

1 The death dive

The Wrights' *Flyer* had an awkward problem, shared with most planes. It stalled. If you tried to fly upwards too steeply, the air moving over the wing flowed less smoothly and slowed down. The wings lost lift and the plane spiralled down and crashed.

In 1912, top test pilot Harry Hawker had the idea of *steepening* the dive as the plane fell. This slowed the plane's speed and allowed the pilot to pull out of the dive. But the only way Hawker could test his hunch was to try it. He was right. Had he been wrong, it would have been less of a hunch and more of a CRUNCH!

2 Stunt flying
Stunt flying attracts the real winged wackos – folk like Lincoln Beachey, nicknamed "the Flying Fool". His tricks included:
• Flying *under* bridges.
• Flying along a street over the heads of passers-by.
• When a group of people climbed a tree to see one of his shows for free, Lincoln buzzed the tree so they fell out.

All of this was deeply dangerous and luckless Lincoln lost his life in 1915 in front of 50,000 people.

Bet you never knew!
In 1910 the Wright brothers set up a flying team to show off their planes, but all but one of the team were killed. The survivor's name was Frank Coffyn.

3 Wing walking
But there's one sport that makes stunt flying sound as sensible as a pair of boring old lace-up shoes. It was started

by potty US pilot Ormer Locklear and to do it you had to walk on the wings of your plane – *while it was in the air*! Or hang from the wheels by your teeth. Or leap to another plane.

Now that's plane crazy, but after the First World War, scores of out-of-work pilots tried it for a living – or dying. And Ormer ended up crashing into a pool of sludgy oil – so he came to a sticky end.

Sorry, readers, you'll have to read this next bit standing on your head. Or you could try flying your plane upside down!

4 Flying upside down

This was pioneered by Russian pilot Petr Nesterov, the first man to loop the loop. The loopy army pilot was rewarded with ten days in prison for risking government property. By the 1930s, upside-down flying was a curious craze and Italian pilot Tito Falconi even flew 420 km from St Louis to Chicago the wrong way up.

Clearly, life for the first pilots was a bit of a gamble and they weren't exactly good risks for life insurance. But at least it was peaceful… In time of war, a pilot's life became even more dangerous…

The deadly demands of war

What is it with humans? No sooner do they invent something than they want to use it to kill each other. In 1917 Orville Wright said that when he and his brother built the world's first plane…

> We thought we were introducing into the world an invention that would make future wars practically impossible…

HOW WRONG THEY WERE! Just look at this…

The fearsome fight for fighting flight

1914–1918 First World War. British, French and American pilots battle with German pilots in the air. The Germans lose because they have fewer planes and pilots.

1939 War breaks out again. The German Air Force rules the skies.

1940 Britain's RAF saves the country from German invasion by shooting down more German planes than it loses.

1940–1942 The Germans bomb British cities instead.

1942–1945 The British and Americans bomb German cities.

1942–1945 American and Japanese planes take off from aircraft carriers to fight vast battles across the Pacific. The Americans win.

In the First World War the life of a fighter pilot was exciting and glorious ... and short. In 1915 a British pilot in France could expect to live just 11 days and pilots were sent into battle with just five hours of flying experience. The British, French or American pilots weren't even allowed parachutes because they might try to escape from their plane rather than fight.

Here's a song by the American squadron in France that you might like sing at school dinners (adding "boy" or "girl" instead of "man").

So stand by your glasses steady
The world is a web of lies
Here's a toast for the dead already
Hurrah for the next man who dies!

Nearly one in three of the brave American pilots were killed – but hopefully your mouldy mashed potato and cabbage aren't quite so dangerous.

But the story of flight in the twentieth century wasn't all doom and destruction. In the 1920s, trail-blazing pilots opened new air routes. These pilots included famous female fliers such as…

• American Amelia Earhart (1898–1937), the first woman to fly the Atlantic in 1928. She was actually a passenger but she amused herself by trying to drop oranges on the head of the captain of a passing ship.

I'M STARVING! HAVEN'T YOU FINISHED PEELING THAT ORANGE YET, AMELIA?

OOPS!

She missed. Four years later she made the trip on her own.

• Briton Amy Johnson (1903–1941), the first woman to fly on her own from Britain to Australia. She also flew the length of Africa and across Asia and lots of other places.

So would you want to sign up for these pioneering flights? Well, they might prove a hair-raising holiday…

HONEST BOB'S HOLIDAYS PRESENTS...

FABULOUS FLIGHTS TO FARAWAY PLACES...
YOU'LL BE THE FIRST ONE TO DO IT!
HEY, IT'S AN ADVENTURE AND
YOU'LL REMEMBER IT FOR THE
REST OF YOUR LIFE (AND THAT
MAY NOT BE VERY LONG –
OOPS, PRETEND I NEVER SAID THAT!)

FREE CRASH COURSE IN FLYING WITH EVERY HOLIDAY SOLD!

1 NEWFOUNDLAND TO IRELAND (1919)

As flown by John Alcock (1892–1919) and Arthur Whitten Brown (1886–1948)

HOPE YOU CAN SWIM

HOPE YOU CAN READ MAPS

- First World War bomber with open cockpit. Lots of lovely fresh freezing air and a hard wooden bench to sit on (it's good for your bum!).
- Experience the first non–stop flight across the Atlantic Ocean. Relive the drama as your radio aerial falls off, so you can't call for help if things go wrong!

- Enjoy lots of exercise as you climb onto the wings to remove ice.

WELL, YOU SAID YOU NEEDED THE BOG!

PLOOP!

- Free sandwiches.
- All this, plus a thrilling crash landing in an Irish bog!

2 THE CHUBBIE MILLER AND BILL LANCASTER WORLD TOUR – Britain to Australia (1928)

It's a thrill a minute as you...

I'M CHUBBIE

AND I'M QUITE THIN

- Find a poisonous snake in your plane in Rangoon.
- Crash in Muntok. (Don't worry if you get a couple of black eyes and a smashed plane – hey, it's all part of the fun!)

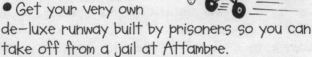

- Get your very own de-luxe runway built by prisoners so you can take off from a jail at Attambre.
- Nearly crash into the Timor Sea and get eaten by sharks. You can write a farewell letter at this point (free stamp).

THE SMALL PRINT – When you get to Australia no one takes much notice of you because another flyer's already made the trip. And you're not allowed to leave your plane until you've been checked for tropical diseases.

3 THE LINDBERGH SPECIAL
– New York to Paris (1927)

Need a little peace and quiet? Well, here's the flight for you! It's only 33 hours but you do it all on your own!

- Lovely break in Paris when you get there – if you get there.
- Your plane has no radio so you don't have to talk to anyone – even if you want to call for help! (Some pilots end up chatting to themselves.)

FANCY A SANDWICH? THANKS, DON'T MIND IF I DO! WHAT'S IN THEM? FISHPASTE. LOVELY!

THE SMALL PRINT
Just make sure you don't fall asleep – or you'll crash and die. By 1927 five pilots had died trying to make this flight.

Lindbergh kept himself awake by slapping his face, bouncing in his seat and sticking his hands out of the window. And by the time he landed in Paris, he probably needed a good night's snooze. He woke up to find himself a world mega-star. He was so incredibly famous...

- The US Government sent a warship to pick him up.
- He got a gold medal from the US Congress.
- He met Orville Wright.

But Charles was so modest and polite that everyone thought he was the best thing since apple pie AND custard.

Lindbergh's famous flight had made flying fab and fashionable like nothing else could. People queued to train as pilots, and passengers queued to fly to the remote parts of the world opened up by pioneer pilots. But what really made passenger flight take off (geddit?) was a new engine that could carry people faster than ever before. Today this engine powers most of the world's passenger planes and we're about to jet off to find out more about it.

Hmm – it's rather noisy. Maybe you'd better put on a pair of these before you read on…

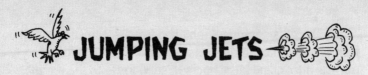

JUMPING JETS

If you've ever flown, the chances are you've flown in a jet plane. This chapter is about how the jet engine was invented and how it changed flying for ever. But first let's check out the basics about this marvellous machine...

Fearsome flight fact file

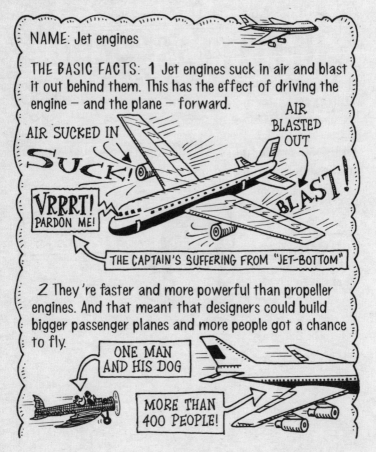

NAME: Jet engines

THE BASIC FACTS: **1** Jet engines suck in air and blast it out behind them. This has the effect of driving the engine – and the plane – forward.

AIR SUCKED IN

AIR BLASTED OUT

SUCK!

BLAST!

VRRRT! PARDON ME!

THE CAPTAIN'S SUFFERING FROM "JET-BOTTOM"

2 They're faster and more powerful than propeller engines. And that meant that designers could build bigger passenger planes and more people got a chance to fly.

ONE MAN AND HIS DOG

MORE THAN 400 PEOPLE!

THE FEARSOME DETAILS: **1** Jet engines can suck in birds and fail. In 1960, 62 people died in Boston, USA, when their plane hit a flock of starlings.

2 Today jet engines are tested by firing dead birds into them with a special cannon. If the engines stop, they fail the test.

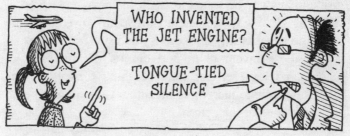

Now, I bet you're wondering who actually came up with the whizzy, wonderful jet engine. Well, as ever in horrible science, the answer is confusingly complicated. It really is a question to stupefy a scientist...

WHO INVENTED THE JET ENGINE?

TONGUE-TIED SILENCE

You see, crowds of inventors had the idea and some of them even designed jet engines that *nearly* worked. I bet if they all met up there'd be a fearsome punch-up over who got the glory...

IT WAS ME!

NEVER!

NO WAY!

IT WAS MY IDEA!

RUBBISH!

TOSH!

The fearsome fight for jet engines

1st century AD Hero, a Greek scientist from Alexandria in Egypt, invents a device that whizzes round, powered by jets of steam. It's not a jet engine but it works in the same way.

1783 Joseph Montgolfier thinks about letting the air out of a balloon so it will whizz off with a rude sound, like a toy balloon. There wasn't enough air pressure in the balloon for this – worse luck!

1791 Inventor John Barber cooks up an engine powered by burning gas. But it's not powerful enough to be much use and anyway he wants to use it in ships.

1837 Sir George Cayley dreams of an air-powered engine – but he never builds it. Too busy as usual, no doubt.

All these inventors missed out on the jumping jet engine, so let's jet our time machine forward to the 1930s, when two incredible inventors were about to grab a bigger slice of the action…

Bet you never knew!
British inventor Frank Whittle (1907–1996) had the idea for the jet engine while studying at flying college in 1929, but his teacher didn't take his brainwave seriously. So, in 1936, Whittle set up his own company to make the new engine, but the British government didn't take him seriously either. Until the Second World War broke out and a fast jet fighter plane suddenly seemed like a good idea…

The incredible thing was that German inventor Hans von Ohain (1911–1998) was also working on the jet engine. The two inventors knew nothing of each other, so we've let them tell their stories separately.

DATE	Frank Whittle's story	Hans von Ohain's story
1939	At last, my government has ordered one plane with my jet engine!	At last, my government has ordered two planes with my jet engine!
1941	My plane flies perfectly.	My two planes fly perfectly.
1944	Hurrah! My jets are fighting the enemy and they're winning.	Grr – my jets are fighting the enemy, but they're dangerous to fly.

HOORAY!!

ERK!

The secret life of the jumping jet engine

And now to find out the innermost secrets of how jet engines work – and a vital new word…

Fearsome expressions

A scientist says…

Do you say…?

Answer:

NO, they're turbines not TURNIPS! A turbine is a sort of spinning fan with angled blades. Turbines produce electricity and power boats and they're vital for jet engines.

It so happens that Professor N Large and Wanda Wye have added a couple of jet engines to their plane. And that's handy because it means we'll be able to see the engines in action. Er, we'd better hurry – Gutzache is just taking off…

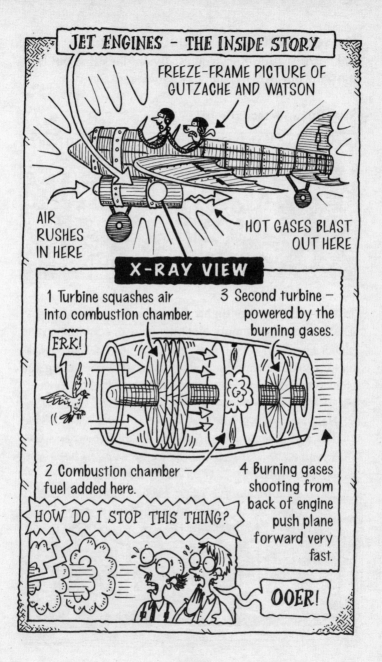

Horrible holidays

Well, if that hadn't put you off flying, let's find out how the jet plane changed the way passengers fly…

Spot the difference competition…

1920s   TODAY

In the 1920s, when flights began between London and Cologne, Germany, only eight passengers could fit on the plane. The plane was so noisy no one could hear you speak, and it shook so alarmingly that the passengers were given cans to throw up in. Oh yes, and the plane had no toilet…

Bet you never knew!
I bet you're wondering how the old-style pilots managed in the days before there were toilets on planes. Well, they held on and if they couldn't… In 1931 US pilot Bobbie Trout used an old coffee can.

290

By the 1950s, passengers could relax on large jet planes (with toilets) and the jet engine provided a smoother flight. But flying could still be a fearsome experience. You had to be *really brave* to fly in some early jets…

Could you be a scientist?
In 1954, Britain's new Comet jets had an annoying habit of falling to bits in the air and crashing.
1 How did scientists find the cause of the crashes?
a) They built a new plane and flew in it.
b) They put the plane in a giant pool and pumped it full of water.
c) They let a bad-tempered elephant wreck the plane and inspected the damage very carefully.

2 What proved to be the problem?
a) The wings were only glued on.
b) The plane was rusty.
c) The square windows had cracked at the corners.

Answers:
1 b) The sides of the plane were too thin. Jet planes fly fastest at heights where the air is thin and causes less drag. But that means air has to be pumped into the cabin so the passengers won't gasp and black out for lack of air to breathe.

… BUT DON'T PUMP TOO MUCH!

THE PASSENGERS ARE COMPLAINING THAT THERE'S TOO MUCH ROOM, CAPTAIN

The changes in air pressure weakened the plane and the scientists found this out by increasing the pressure of the water on the plane.

2 c) And the weakest point was the corner of the windows.

Bet you never knew!
Modern jets are far stronger. For example, the sides of a jumbo jet are 19 cm thick and the windows are toughened glass as thick as your fist.

Teacher's tea-break teaser

Tap lightly on the staffroom door. When your teacher appears, smile sweetly and ask them…

Your teacher will crossly inform you that a Boeing 747 *is* a jumbo jet. This is true – jumbo jet is a nickname for the plane – but you can say…

By the 1970s flying was an everyday event – in 1977 nearly two-thirds of Americans had flown … in the previous year! And air travel has continued to grow. Today, jets fly millions of passengers all over the world. And there's even a choice of jet engines…

• Ordinary plain old turbo-jet engines, like the ones on Gutzache's plane.

• Turbo-fan engines, used in large jets. A fan draws air into the engine and wafts some air round the combustion chamber to keep it cool.

• Turbo-prop or prop-fan engines, which combine turbines with propellers.

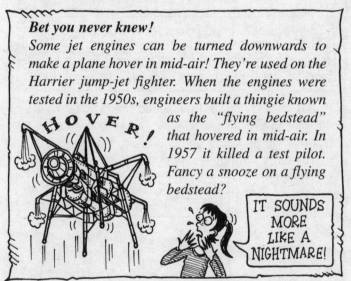

Bet you never knew!

Some jet engines can be turned downwards to make a plane hover in mid-air! They're used on the Harrier jump-jet fighter. When the engines were tested in the 1950s, engineers built a thingie known as the "flying bedstead" that hovered in mid-air. In 1957 it killed a test pilot. Fancy a snooze on a flying bedstead?

IT SOUNDS MORE LIKE A NIGHTMARE!

And by the 1970s there was another type of plane to fly in. A plane that travelled faster than your VOICE and made the jumbo jet look like a slug with a wooden leg. Yes, this next bit is sure to take the words out of your mouth…

Fearsome flight fact file

NAME: Supersonic jets

THE BASIC FACTS: 1 Imagine your teacher telling you to go home early. The sound of her voice actually reaches your ears at 1,220 km per hour. And that's only slightly slower than the class leaving the classroom.

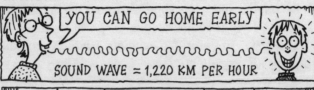

YOU CAN GO HOME EARLY

SOUND WAVE ≈ 1,220 KM PER HOUR

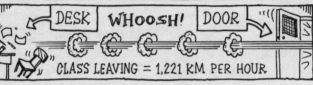

DESK WHOOSH! DOOR

CLASS LEAVING = 1,221 KM PER HOUR

2 Jets that fly faster than sound travel faster than the air can get out of the way. The air builds up in front of the plane like a wall – it's called the sound barrier. Once through this wall, the flight is smoother.

STAND BY FOR A BIG BANG...

YOU MEAN, THE SONIC BOOM AS WE BREAK THE SOUND BARRIER?

NO, THE LOUD BOOM WHEN WE HIT THAT MOUNTAIN

3 Supersonic planes are streamlined to reduce drag. They have swept-back, "delta-shaped" wings so the wing hits the sound barrier at an angle rather than straight on. This makes the ride less bumpy.

G de Havilland

Chuck Yeager

Watch the birdie!
5 Birds that fly fast

WE HAWKS HAVE WINGS SHAPED LIKE A JET.

ITS SHAPE GIVES ME LIFT WITHOUT TOO MUCH DRAG...

LIKE SOME JETS, I CAN FOLD MY WINGS BACK FOR A MORE STREAMLINED SHAPE.

SWEPT-BACK WING

POINTED SHAPE

THEN I DIVE AT 180 KM PER HOUR. OK, SO IT'S NOT AS FAST AS A JET...

ERK! BUT IT'S FAST ENOUGH TO CATCH ME!

But you could interest your parents in a vintage classic plane from the 1970s. Concorde was a supersonic passenger jet developed in Britain and France, and it so happens that Honest Bob's got one for sale...

HONEST BOB'S PLANE PRODUCTS PRESENTS...

CONCORDE They don't make Concordes like they used to. Well, they don't make them at all! But just look what you get for your £50,999,999 (bring the money in a suitcase and don't ask awkward questions).
Top speed = 2,333 km per hour.
Gold-plated windows cut down on harmful rays from the sun.

PARACHUTE TO SLOW IT DOWN FOR LANDING

NOSE DROOPS ON TAKEOFF AND LANDING SO THE PILOTS CAN SEE WHERE THEY'RE GOING

MY NOSE ISN'T DROOPY!

NO TAIL PLANE

ELEVONS = COMBINED AILERONS AND ELEVATORS

The vital facts that somehow slipped Bob's mind

1 Concorde was so noisy that it was banned from flying over many countries.

2 In a bid to make the plane quieter, it flew at 800 km per hour over land. But then it used fuel eight times more quickly than a normal jet plane.

A fantastic future in the air?

So what do the next 50 years hold for the future of flight? Er, well, I'd love to give you the lowdown on tomorrow's high-flyers, but sadly I can't. My crystal ball is cracked and my tea leaves have dribbled down the sink... And anyway, the fearsome fight for flight is full of obscure inventors who suddenly pop up with machines that no one believed possible.

But we can take a look at some cutting-edge, state-of-the-art aircraft that might just become more common in years to come. They're built from new materials called composites (com-po-sits). These substances are made up of two different materials such as carbon and kevlar, and they're very light and strong. So they're a plane-designer's dream...

Honest Bob is selling the planes, but he's just bumped his head and now he's a changed man... He's actually become honest!

EVEN-MORE HONEST BOB'S PLANE PRODUCTS PRESENTS...

"Bob telling the truth? It ain't natural!" Bob's mum

THESE PLANES HONESTLY ARE THE BUSINESS (AND I MEAN THAT MOST SINCERELY!)

1 THE HELIOS SOLAR-POWERED PLANE

GULP! WHAT HAPPENS WHEN THE SUN GOES IN?

- Stays up on its own, powered only by the sun for weeks on end.

- It's got lots of solar cells to make electricity from sunlight.

- Lots of engines – just in case some fall off.

- 76-metre wingspan for maximum lift.

Price: To be honest, I think it's a bit more than you can afford.

2 THE GLOBAL HAWK

If you're into radio planes, this is the machine for you!

TEATIME!

HANG ON, MUM. I'M FLYING OVER RUSSIA

• You can fly it from your computer on the other side of the world.

• Super-sensitive spy cameras can spot your teacher's underpants on the washing line from 74 km away. It's your very own spy in the sky!

• As used by the US military.

• It's even got a self-destruct programme.

Price: I'll do you the cheapest price I can – but it's still a bit steep!

3 THE GOSSAMER ALBATROSS PEDAL-POWERED PLANE

CHOMP! MUNCH! HMM, NICE CHOC!

HE'S FILLING HIS ENGINE WITH FUEL

• Lovely pedal-powered plane made of plastic and piano wire.

• 30-metre wing span for maximum lift.

• Three-metre propeller powered by your pedals.

• Guaranteed not to fly more than a few metres in the air, so you won't get hurt if it crashes.

Price: Unlike the plane ... it's too high!

Yes, at last humans had achieved the ultimate dream of muscle-powered flight. But hold on ... a human flying from Crete? Isn't that how the fearsome fight for flight began?

THANKS FOR REMINDING ME!

EPILOGUE: FATEFUL FLIGHT

As Jacques Charles lifted off in his hydrogen balloon in 1785, wise old American scientist Benjamin Franklin (1706–1790) was among the crowd. A man next to him asked, "What's the use of it?"
Franklin replied…

WHAT'S THE USE OF A NEWBORN BABY?

I BEG YOUR PARDON?

No, silly! Franklin didn't mean that flying would only be good for eating, dribbling, crying and other unmentionable baby behaviour. He meant that, like a baby, flight was the start of something new and exciting. Something that would grow and grow. And boy was he right!

Flying has proved to be the biggest success story in the history of the world. It's changed the lives of countless millions of people in an incredibly short time…

• The first engine-powered plane flight happened in 1903. Just 44 years later, humans were flying faster than sound. It all happened inside a human lifetime.

• Just five people saw the *Flyer's* first flight. There was no airfield except a pair of rails that cost $5.

• Today there are airports all over the planet and the biggest ones, such as King Khalid Airport in Saudi Arabia, are larger than small countries. (It's four times bigger than the entire island of Bermuda.)

• The *Flyer* flew no higher than a budgie and no faster than a racing bicycle.

• Today's fastest planes can zoom 16 km in the air at the speed of a rifle bullet. In 2004 US scientists tested a robot plane than could fly at *seven times* the speed of sound.

• In 1903 most letters were carried on carts pulled by wheezy old horses. Today a letter can sent anywhere on Earth and arrive in days by air. And where letters go, so can people.

Planes … the good news
1 Flying has helped millions of people visit new parts of the world and make new friends in other countries.
2 Flying has brought food and medicines to hungry and sick people in disaster areas.
3 Scientists have gained the chance to study pollution and rocks and mountains and wild animals from the air. In terms of what flying can do, the sky really is the limit and yet … and yet.

Planes … the fearsome news

1 As more and more people fly, airports are getting overcrowded.

2 There's more noise and more pollution and more danger of planes bashing into each other as they wait to land.

3 Planes have killed thousands of people by bombing.

People paid a fearsome price to fly. Experts reckon that even before the *Flyer's* first flight, 200 men were killed trying to fly with wacko wings, barmy balloons and grisly gliders. But then flying is a bit like science. You can't say it's either good or bad – it's what you do with it that counts. Happy Horrible Science, everyone!

HORRIBLE SCIENCE

Science with the squishy bits left in!

Ugly Bugs • Blood, Bones and Body Bits
Nasty Nature • Chemical Chaos • Fatal Forces
Sounds Dreadful • Evolve or Die • Vicious Veg
Disgusting Digestion • Bulging Brains
Frightening Light • Shocking Electricity
Deadly Diseases • Microscopic Monsters
Killer Energy • The Body Owner's Handbook
The Terrible Truth About Time
Space, Stars and Slimy Aliens • Painful Poison
The Fearsome Fight For Flight • Angry Animals
Measly Medicine

Suffering Scientists
Explosive Experiments
The Awfully Big Quiz Book
Really Rotten Experiments

Two horrible books in one
Ugly Bugs and Nasty Nature
Blood, Bones and Body Bits and Chemical Chaos
Frightening Light and Sounds Dreadful
Bulging Brains and Disgusting Digestion
Microscopic Monsters and Deadly Diseases
Killer Energy and Shocking Electricity

Colour books
The Stunning Science of Everything
Dangerous Dinosaurs Jigsaw Book